THE GREAT CHEVAUCHÉE

John of Gaunt's Raid on France 1373

DAVID NICOLLE

First published in Great Britain in 2011 by Osprey Publishing,
Midland House, West Way, Botley, Oxford, OX2 0PH, UK
44–02 23rd St, Suite 219, Long Island City, NY 11101, USA

E-mail: info@ospreypublishing.com

A CIP catalogue record for this book is available from the British Library

Print ISBN: 978 1 84908 247 1
PDF e-book ISBN: 978 1 84908 248 8

Page layout by Bounford.com, Cambridge, UK
Index by Margaret Vaudrey
Typeset in Sabon
Maps by Bounford.com
Artist: Peter Dennis
BEVs: Donato Spedaliere/Alina Illustrazioni
Originated by PPS Grasmere Ltd, Leeds, UK
Printed in China through Worldrprint Ltd

11 12 13 14 15   10 9 8 7 6 5 4 3 2 1

Osprey Publishing is supporting the Woodland Trust, the UK's leading
woodland conservation charity, by funding the dedication of trees.

www.ospreypublishing.com

DEDICATION

For my father, Maurice Patrick ('Pat') Nicolle; proud Englishman and lover
of France, who considered the 14th century to be the most interesting of
them all.

CONTENTS

INTRODUCTION

There is a tendency in the English-speaking world to envisage the Hundred Years War between England and France as a sequence of dramatic English victories in battle followed by somewhat puzzling defeat. Certainly the first phase of the conflict was marked by successes that have burned themselves into the country's collective memory, most notably Crécy in 1346 and Poitiers in 1356. Then came the Treaty of Brétigny in 1360, which left a third of France under the recognized rule of King Edward III of England.

Yet by the end of the 14th century, English rule had been reduced to a few small – in some cases tiny – coastal enclaves. How this happened tends to be glossed over in British history books. It represented a collapse marked by few battles on land, none of which involved large armies, and one major naval defeat, which is even more embarrassing for a proud maritime nation. On the other hand the English did not simply roll over. In fact the second phase of the Hundred Years War, from 1369 until 1396, saw several major efforts by the English, on land and sea, to restore their position in France. Perhaps the most ambitious, remarkable and indeed heroic was the Great Chevauchée commanded by John of Gaunt, the Duke of Lancaster, in 1373. Yet it also failed in its primary objectives, and was followed by an English collapse in Aquitaine.

A number of other events had an even greater impact on the course of these first two phases of the Hundred Years War. Above all there was the Black Death, a series of epidemics of bubonic plague that wrought havoc across much of the known world. Reaching France in 1348 and most of England the following year, the plague returned again and again, the last major outbreaks being in 1369 and 1375. John of Gaunt's Great Chevauchée was therefore launched between two epidemics. Military casualties were tiny when compared to those caused by the Black Death, and although plague mortality was less among the elite than amongst ordinary people it was nevertheless still high, leading to a reshaping of the aristocratic social and military fabric in both countries. Indeed it was

often necessary to promote new men and families to aristocratic status with its attendant military obligations. The economic impact of the Black Death also meant that the value of many aristocratic estates, even those of royal families, fell and had not recovered at the time John of Gaunt was desperately searching for money to finance his ambitious new campaign in France.

France had been the richest country in Europe at the start of the Hundred Years War and despite defeats and plagues its rulers still seem to have had relatively little difficulty raising money for increasingly professional, mercenary and expensive armies. In fact it seems that the continuation of the war often benefited the surviving nobility and urban oligarchies, as well as the government bureaucracy in France. But it was of no benefit to the peasantry, amongst whom it came to be said that '*Les bois sont venus en France avec les Anglais*' (Forests came to France with the English) because a steep decline in the rural economy led to an increase in wooded areas at the expense of agricultural land.[1]

Yet it is interesting to note that the war had little impact on the level of crime in France, many violent crimes actually being acts of resistance by supporters of one side or the other. What is clear is that the conflict enabled the French legal system to strengthen ideas of loyalty to the crown rather than to local lords. Indeed in both England and France kings and their governments increasingly expected unflinching obedience in what might be interpreted as the dawn of modern nationalism. Significant cultural changes also had a military impact by changing attitudes amongst military elites.

In England, for example, French remained a language of culture and gentility even in the later 14th century. However it was now a prestigious but

The Tuchins, who rose in revolt across much of southern France in the 1360s, reflected the desperation of the people and the ravages caused by war. The rugged nature of the terrain, such as that seen here at Pont du Rastel, also meant that decades passed before government authority was restored. (Author's photograph)

---

1 Favreau, R., 'L'enquête pontificale 1373 sur les Hospitaliers dans la diocèse de Saintes', in A. Luttrell & L. Pressouyre (eds), *La Commanderie*, Paris (2002), p.271

The battle of La Rochelle, in which an English fleet was defeated by France's Castilian allies within sight of these harbour towers triggered a collapse of English power in south-western France, which in turn prompted John of Gaunt's epic raid of 1373. (Author's photograph)

foreign tongue, rather like Latin. Even amongst the higher aristocracy, who were so proud of their Norman or French origins, the stumbling Anglo-Norman French of the nobility was becoming something of a joke, especially as the Hundred Years War encouraged increasing francophobia across England. Meanwhile English was establishing its superiority among the country gentry and lower aristocracy, despite the fact that its use was hampered by a huge variety of dialects and spellings. Chaucer noted this problem in his great poem *Troilus and Criseyde*, which he completed just over ten years after the Great Chevauchée:

> And for ther is so greet diversitee
> In English and in wryting of our tonge,
> So preye I god that noon miswryte thee,
> Ne thee mismetre for defaute of tonge.[2]

In England, these years similarly saw a significant rise in the power of Parliament, though the institution itself could hardly yet be called democratic. In the year of the Great Chevauchée the merchants of England proclaimed that Parliament rather than various mercantile assemblies represented their wishes, and in 1373 or 1374, according to the *Eulogium*

---

2 Chaucer, Geoffrey (W.W. Skeat ed., S. Boston tr.), *Troilus & Criseyde*, London (1990), verse 257

Historiarum, a great council took place in Westminster in the presence of Edward III's eldest son, the Black Prince, and the Archbishop of Canterbury concerning the validity of papal taxation. Whether it really took place is a matter of debate, and the story might simply be anti-papal propaganda.

Less than a decade later southern England was convulsed by the Peasants' Revolt, but by then France had suffered more prolonged violence from the 'lower orders'. The bloody Jacquerie uprising of 1358 was worst in areas north of Paris and stemmed largely from dissatisfaction with an aristocracy that had failed in its primary roles as defender of the kingdom and upkeeper of law and order. It involved many other groups of society in addition to the traditional agricultural peasantry and, although the Jacquerie was soon crushed, it had stirred up terrifying class hatreds. The Tuchin revolts of the 1360s were more prolonged but were confined to the south of the country. Having flared up in the Haute Auvergne about 1360, these revolts eventually spread to towns around 1378, and were seen across much of the Languedoc. The Tuchins reached their peak in the winter of 1382–83 before finally being suppressed in 1385. By then, of course, the Great Chevauchée had not only marched right through the worst-hit heartlands of the Tuchin revolt but, by spreading still more devastation, disruption and despair, had contributed substantially to its causes.

ORIGINS

The origins of the Great Chevauchée lie in the period of relentless English setbacks from the failure of the Treaty of Brétigny to the fall of La Rochelle in September 1372. Brétigny had recognized the English king, Edward III, as the sovereign ruler of about one third of France, and not as a vassal of the French king as had previously been the case for 'English' territory in France. King Jean 'the Good' of France, having been captured at the battle of Poitiers, eventually agreed to the Treaty of Brétigny but died four years later. He was succeeded by his son Charles V, who, though cautious and unwarlike, wanted revenge for the humiliation of Brétigny without the risks of full-scale war.

Within a year of coming to the throne he won a significant victory over King Charles of Navarre who, like the English monarchs of earlier centuries, owned large territories within France and had resisted the authority of the French king. However this was promptly followed by a less successful campaign in Brittany, where Charles's most famous commander, Bertrand du Guesclin, was captured – not for the first time in his remarkable career – by an Anglo-Breton army at the battle of Auray.

Despite this setback, the pro-English Duke Jean IV of Brittany was for a while driven out. Nevertheless, this complex conflict, known as the War of Breton Succession (1341–65) ended with Jean IV returning as Duke and coming to terms with Charles V. The English and French kings next supported rival claimants to the crown of León and Castile in Spain, where they fought another 'proxy war'. Meanwhile the English were committed to the unprofitable occupation of extensive territories in France, where their presence was widely, though not universally, resented.

As if this was not enough, there was further Anglo-French competition in Flanders, which was currently going through one of the most tumultuous periods in its tumultuous history. While most of Flanders was either ruled or dominated by France, within the country the wealthy and economically advanced cities dominated the rural countryside. Indeed Flanders had much in common with early Renaissance Italy in political, economic and social, if not yet cultural, terms. Like much of Italy, much of Flanders was also hugely

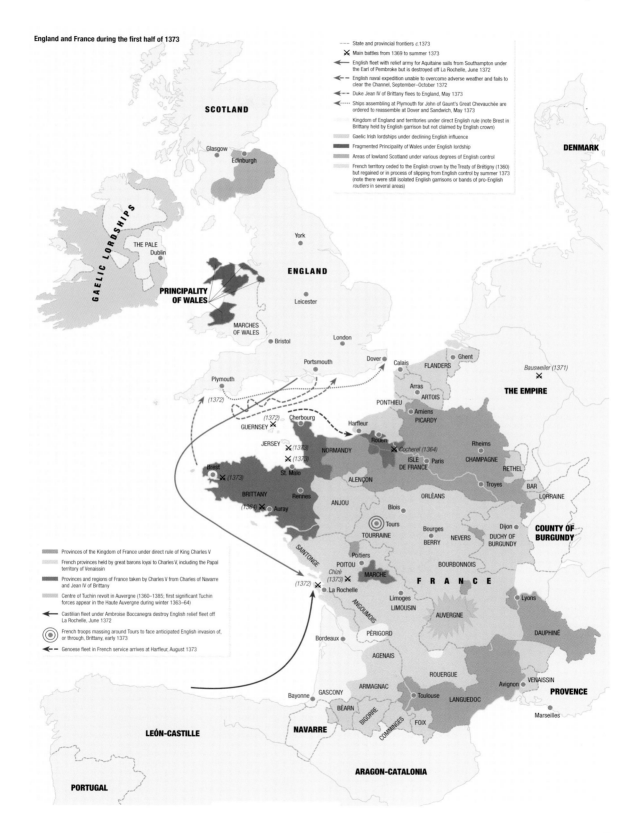

England and France during the first half of 1373

- - - - - State and provincial frontiers *c.*1373
- ✕ Main battles from 1369 to summer 1373
- ← English fleet with relief army for Aquitaine sails from Southampton under the Earl of Pembroke but is destroyed off La Rochelle, June 1372
- ←‑ ‑ English naval expedition unable to overcome adverse weather and fails to clear the Channel, September–October 1372
- ←·‑·‑ Duke Jean IV of Brittany flees to England, May 1373
- ←···· Ships assembling at Plymouth for John of Gaunt's Great Chevauchée are ordered to reassemble at Dover and Sandwich, May 1373
- Kingdom of England and territories under direct English rule (note Brest in Brittany held by English garrison but not claimed by English crown)
- Gaelic Irish lordships under declining English influence
- Fragmented Principality of Wales under English lordship
- Areas of lowland Scotland under various degrees of English control
- French territory ceded to the English crown by the Treaty of Brétigny (1360) but regained or in process of slipping from English control by summer 1373 (note there were still isolated English garrisons or bands of pro-English *routiers* in several areas)

SCOTLAND

Glasgow
Edinburgh

GAELIC LORDSHIPS

THE PALE
Dublin

York

ENGLAND

PRINCIPALITY OF WALES

Leicester

MARCHES OF WALES

Bristol

London

Plymouth
(1372)

Portsmouth

Dover

Calais
FLANDERS
Ghent

Bausweiler (1371)
✕

THE EMPIRE

DENMARK

Arras
ARTOIS
PONTHIEU
Amiens
PICARDY

Cherbourg
GUERNSEY *(1372)* ✕
Harfleur
Rouen

JERSEY ✕ *(1373)*
✕ *(1373)*

NORMANDY
✕ Cocherel *(1364)*
ISLE DE FRANCE
Paris
Rheims
CHAMPAGNE
RETHEL

Brest
✕ *(1373)*
St. Malo

BRITTANY
Rennes
(1364) ✕ Auray

ALENÇON

ANJOU

Troyes
BAR
LORRAINE

ORLÉANS

Blois

Tours
TOURRAINE

Bourges
BERRY
NEVERS
Dijon
DUCHY OF BURGUNDY
COUNTY OF BURGUNDY

SANTONGE

Poitiers
POITOU
Chizè
(1373) ✕
MARCHE

BOURBONNOIS

F R A N C E

(1372) ✕
La Rochelle

Limoges
LIMOUSIN

AUVERGNE

Lyons

DAUPHINÉ

ANGOUMOIS

Bordeaux

PÉRIGORD

AGENAIS

Avignon
VENAISSIN
PROVENCE

Marseilles

Bayonne
GASCONY

ARMAGNAC

Toulouse
LANGUEDOC

ROUERGUE

LEÓN-CASTILLE

NAVARRE

BÉARN
BIGORRE
COMMINGES
FOIX

ARAGON-CATALONIA

PORTUGAL

Provinces of the Kingdom of France under direct rule of King Charles V

French provinces held by great barons loyal to Charles V, including the Papal territory of Venaissin

Provinces and regions of France taken by Charles V from Charles of Navarre and Jean IV of Brittany

Centre of Tuchin revolt in Auvergne (1360–1385; first significant Tuchin forces appear in the Haute Auvergne during winter 1363–64)

← Castilian fleet under Ambroise Boccanegra destroy English relief fleet off La Rochelle, June 1372

◎ French troops massing around Tours to face anticipated English invasion of, or through, Brittany, early 1373

←‑ Genoese fleet in French service arrives at Harfleur, August 1373

rich, which was one reason why both England and France competed for influence or outright domination.

Factional and guild violence was particularly serious in Ghent, where the Guild of Weavers had been firmly in control since around 1361, excluding their rivals the Guild of Fullers from power. However, the fullers tended to be backed by the Count of Flanders, Louis de Male, who gave them a substantial pay increase when they struck for higher wages in 1373 – the year of the Great Chevauchée. Added to this toxic mix of local tensions along France's frontiers, Charles V of France was eager to expand his family's powerbase and strongly supported his younger brother Philip as Duke of Burgundy. To avoid opposition from Louis de Male, Charles even handed back the small but strategic territories of Lille, Douai and Orchies, which the French crown had won early in the 14th century. These lay close to the Great Chevauchée's line of march.

Above all Charles wanted to have a strong and friendly power in this region, capable of stopping the English from landing an army on what is now the Belgian coast. Charles V's greatest success came in June 1369 when his brother Philip of Burgundy won the hand of Margaret of Flanders, heir to the County, who had also been courted by an English prince – none other than Edward III's second son, John of Gaunt Earl of Lancaster and soon to be commander of the Great Chevauchée. One may be tempted to think that the forthcoming confrontation between John of Gaunt and Philip of Burgundy had a personal as well as a strategic element. Nor might it have been a coincidence that John of Gaunt seemed keen to show the flag near the frontiers of the German Empire. Here an important ally, Duke Eduard I of Guelders, had recently been killed at the battle of Baesweiler, near Aachen.

Of course not everything had been going in favour of King Charles V. Large swathes of France were still infested with *compagnies d'aventure* – the name generally given to more or less coherently organized bands of redundant soldiers or *routiers* who had turned brigand after the Treaty of Brétigny. Interestingly, there are no references to Genoese crossbowmen or other Italians in these *companies*, the strictly professional Italian mercenaries having simply looked for work elsewhere once their contracts with the French crown ended. A large part of Charles V's military effort was, in fact, directed towards curbing or expelling these unemployed soldiers from the country. In this Bertrand du Guesclin proved to be highly effective, having himself previously been a *routier*.

One region which continued to suffer particularly badly from the *compagnies d'aventure* was the Auvergne. The depredations, despair and widespread famine they caused had been major factors in the outbreak of the Tuchin revolt. In fact the first uprising came in the aftermath of the more official havoc caused by a chevauchée by the English commander Robert Knolles and his lieutenant Hugues of Calverly in 1359. These two forces were then threatened by a French army led by the Duke of Bourbon, which resulted in the English and their local allies dispersing across the Haute-Auvergne.

Then came the Treaty of Brétigny and supposedly peace. The remnants of that chevauchée were instead joined by newly unemployed English and

Gascon soldiers from Aquitaine. Together they installed themselves in various parts of the highlands and were still there when John of Gaunt's Great Chevauchée appeared late in 1373. By then responsibility for the defence of French-ruled Auvergne had passed from its previous lieutenant-general, Duke Louis of Anjou, to his brother Duke Jean of Berry. Most of these men would soon play their part in the epic of the Great Chevauchée. The Tuchins were also still on the scene. Though now living as dispossessed bandits and outlaws, they included people from a wide section of French society: peasants, workers, artisans, small merchants, even elements from the urban bourgeoisies and minor aristocracy.

It was against this already disturbed background that in 1368 the Black Prince, as English governor and Duke of Aquitaine, demanded higher taxes. The estates or local representative body of Aquitaine complained both to the king of England and to the king of France. Strictly speaking, according to the terms of the Treaty of Brétigny, Charles no longer had any jurisdiction within Aquitaine but his legal advisers informed him that – because some terms of the treaty had not been completely fulfilled by the English – the Treaty of Brétigny was not yet valid. By agreeing to listen to appeals by two *appellants* from Aquitaine, Charles V made a clash with the Black Prince inevitable.

Then on 30 November 1369 Charles went further, 'confiscating' Aquitaine on the grounds that the English had not carried out their side of the Treaty. By then French military preparations were well advanced, while the English were clearly caught unprepared. The French king's brother, the Duke of Anjou, had already won support from some of the lesser aristocracy of Gascony, without whom the English position in Aquitaine would be practically untenable. Though the now aged and ill King Edward III of England wanted a peaceful resolution, his warlike but also unwell son the Black Prince reportedly responded to a summons from King Charles V with the words: 'We shall go to Paris, but with helmets on and sixty thousand troops behind us.' In reality, no such English army was available, but the second phase of the Hundred Years War was now on.

Du Guesclin, having been ransomed after the battle of Auray, was now recalled from Spain to become 'Constable', or most senior military commander in France, where he was joined by Charles V's brothers, Duke Louis of Anjou, Duke Jean of Berry and Duke Philip of Burgundy. King Charles V's characteristic caution and desire to keep all options open had, however, led to a peculiarly medieval example of courtesy. In April 1369, even as his troops were invading English-ruled Pontieu and were advancing in Rouergue and Quercy, the French king sent 50 'pipes' of wine from Beaune to his 'dear cousin', King Edward III.

In stark terms, the years 1369 to 1396 saw England fail to maintain the military dominance it had previously won, despite major efforts that involved huge expense and large numbers of troops. The first six years were characterized by French successes on land and a resounding Castilian naval victory on behalf of France in 1372. Then came several years of remarkable French naval success, during which many parts of the English coast were

King Charles V of France giving a banquet to the German Emperor Charles IV in the Grande Salle of the Palais de la Cité in Paris, as illustrated in the *Grandes Chroniques de France* made in Paris around 1378–80 (Bibliothèque Nationale, Ms. Fr. 2813, f. 473v, Paris)

23 JUNE 1372

Battle of La Rochelle

raided. But a French intervention in Scotland in 1385 failed, a French campaign to invade England in 1386 never took place, and a truce was once again agreed in 1396.

This interesting conflict has nevertheless been largely ignored by English historians, and was misunderstood by some of those who did refer to it. A.H. Burne, respected military historian of the Hundred Years War, merely stated: 'In this war nothing worthy of the name of battle was fought. This was because French armies refused to meet English armies in the field, acting under the strict orders of their king. English armies in consequence were able to roam the country at will, while the French confined themselves to sieges.

The war is thus rather lacking in military interest, for there was remarkably little actual fighting.'[3]

In fact Burne missed the point. This phase of the Hundred Years War was typified by the fall, one after another, of English-held fortresses that were supposed to guard Aquitaine. Meanwhile frustrated English chevauchées rampaged across France, unable to bring French armies to the sort of war-winning battles that had given England victory in the first phase of the conflict. At the same time English attempts to get sufficient forces to Aquitaine to restore the situation also failed, though for more varied reasons. As C.T. Allmand, a more recent military historian of this period, has put it, 'The nature of the conflict fought in the 1370s was to be very different from that of earlier decades, and its effects more dramatic. The French were not unprepared, and almost immediately took the offensive.'[4] The greatly enlarged English territories in France had long and exposed frontiers 'vulnerable to small mobile forces which the French now used to excellent effect'. The English might still have believed in their inherent, even God-given, military superiority, but their leaders nevertheless had a genuine fear that the French might imitate the English archery that had won at Crécy and Poitiers. Consequently the export of bows and arrows was banned, and since 1365 even the archers had been forbidden to leave England without royal licence.

21–23 MARCH 1373

Battle of Chizé

The Angers Apocalypse tapestry, in which King Edward III of England and his sons are represented as demon-horses, ridden and led by the Devil. It was commissioned by Duke Louis of Anjou and was woven by Nicholas Bataille around 1380. (Angers castle museum)

---

3 Burne, A.H., *The Agincourt War: A Military History of the Latter Part of the Hundred Years War from 1369 to 1453*, London (1956), p.20

4 Allmand, C.T., *The Hundred Years War: England and France at War c.1300–c.1450*, Cambridge (1988), p.22

INITIAL STRATEGY

English efforts to counter French strategy in the early 1370s had proved ineffective, much to the surprise of an English nation that had become accustomed to victory. In return for considerable money, but relatively little blood, the English had achieved little. They were forced to fight an essentially defensive war of fortifications against an enemy who avoided major battlefield confrontations yet regained territory, firstly those provinces ceded by the Treaty of Brétigny, and then most of Aquitaine, which had, of course, been held by England's Plantagenet ruling dynasty for centuries.

The only offensive strategy seemingly available to the English was the traditional chevauchée. John of Gaunt's campaign in 1373 would fall into this category, but its size and scope might suggest that it had broader aims than merely devastation and the hope of bringing a significant French army to battle. According to the chronicler Jean Froissart, whose knowledge of these events was detailed and personal, the Great Chevauchée had been planned for over three years. Such a massive enterprise might have been intended to reverse the whole course of the war. It has even been suggested that John of Gaunt hoped not only to defeat Charles V's army and bring a large relief force to Aquitaine, but that this would then serve as the nucleus of a larger army that could cross the Pyrenees to place John of Gaunt on the throne that he claimed – namely that of León and Castile. Closer study of the original sources provides no evidence for such a plan, though we cannot know if John of Gaunt had such an ambitious idea in the back of his mind.

What the sources do show is that John of Gaunt spent much of 1372 in his palace of the Savoy, overlooking the River Thames between the cities of London and Westminster. There he was involved in detailed military and diplomatic preparations, consulting with King Edward III and his Royal Council, conducting a vigorous diplomatic campaign to win Spanish allies for his Castilian claims but at the same time giving priority to England's interests in France. From early in the year he 'indentured', or signed up, increasing numbers of captains and their troops, all of whom agreed to muster for the forthcoming campaign at the specified time and place.

King Edward was now too frail to take command and for a while it seemed as if the Black Prince would be in charge, but he proved too ill even to take part. The catastrophic English naval defeat off La Rochelle in June also led to changes in the plan, with the English now giving priority to challenging the victorious Castilian fleet. For example, on 1 July 1372 John of Gaunt himself undertook to serve for a year 'on and over the sea', then ten days later he issued 'letters of summons', which ordered his own retinue to assemble for service at sea without horses. However, the specified embarkation port of Sandwich on the eastern tip of Kent suggested a naval operation in the Channel rather than the Bay of Biscay. Clearly the strategy was still evolving and, as it turned out, the Great Chevauchée would not be the only English operation in 1373.

Here it is worth noting that most English chevauchées started from Calais. As a result the neighbouring French regions of Artois, Picardy, Champagne and the Ile de France were not only the worst hit but now also amongst the best-defended areas, especially in terms of castles and urban fortifications. English armies had a ferocious reputation for their capabilities in chevauchée warfare, where the brutality of ordinary English soldiers seems to have been unsurpassed, yet English armies had a poor reputation for siege warfare where they only occasionally succeeded. A generation or more of success in full-scale battle apparently encouraged the English to seek major confrontations and, in the words of the time, 'to let God decide'. For their part the French, or at least their leaders, having suffered several massive defeats in large battles, had learned to play by different rules. It should also be noted that the traditional, now almost legendary, effectiveness of the English archer with his now inaccurately named 'longbow', was actually quite limited. Terrifyingly powerful in ranged battles of massed ranks, he was much less useful in sieges and was almost useless on a chevauchée if enemy forces chose not to come face-to-face.

Though it could serve as a launching pad for chevauchées like that of 1373, Calais' surrounding enclave was so small that all munitions, materials for fortifications, food and money had to be sent from England. The size of its garrison varied according to the military and political situation, but would almost certainly have been large in 1373. Meanwhile Calais was also an important intelligence-gathering base, though perhaps one where French agents were also active. Given the fact that Charles V and his senior commanders were clearly informed about John of Gaunt's plans in 1373, the widespread fear of spies during this period may have been justified. Unfortunately in England it went hand in hand with increasing hostility towards foreigners, particularly foreign clergy and friars. One of Edward III's laws actually ordered innkeepers to search guests and to report on them, while high-ranking visitors were routinely interrogated by the Royal Council. Fear of spies was similarly great in France, ambassadors being widely disliked and even those arranging the ransom or exchange of prisoners being suspect because they had contact with the enemy.

Meanwhile the French offensive in Aquitaine continued, culminating with Bertrand du Guesclin's small but significant victory over an Anglo-Breton

The nave of the Cathedral of Saint-André in Bordeaux, where John of Gaunt is said to have announced his withdrawal from Aquitaine to the assembled nobility of that fast-shrinking province. (Author's photograph)

army at the battle of Chizé between 21 and 23 March 1373. However, the fact that English archers on one side and French crossbowmen on the other played only a minor role meant that the battle of Chizé may not have been typical. The total victory of English bowmen at the battle of Agincourt was still to come, 42 years later. The subsequent fall of the English-held town of Chizé to Du Guesclin effectively completed the French reconquest of Poitou, which may have been less important than the moral impact of the first significant French battlefield victory against a largely English army for several decades.

The day before announcing this victory, King Charles V granted Duke Louis of Bourbon and Constable Du Guesclin authority to negotiate a change of allegiance with any town or fortress in Guyenne – the very heartland of what remained of English territory in Aquitaine. The reinvigorated French now went on to take Niort, Lusignan and Mortemer. Cognac and John of Gaunt's own town of Roche-sur-Yon had already fallen, while the coastal region of Saintonge was as good as taken. Chauvigni, Lussac, Moncontour and Sainte-Sévère fell in August, while besieged Thouars agreed to surrender to the French if no help arrived by 30 September.

For the English, the decline of their naval power led to a change in their view of the English Channel. Having been a route to continental Europe since before Roman times, it increasingly came to be seen as a huge defensive moat, separating England from its neighbours – an attitude that hardened over subsequent centuries and is sadly still strong today.

This naval dimension was so important at the time of the Great Chevauchée that it governed the campaign's entire strategy. The main role of the English fleet, insofar as it yet existed, was to provide armed transports to carry armies to France and protect smaller ships similarly engaged. Naval technology and ship design were more advanced than is generally recognized but, unlike the maritime powers of the Mediterranean and more recently the Iberian peninsula, England had very few oared warships capable of much speed or manoeuvre. France was also a relative newcomer in this field. Most English and French ships were designed as transports and as yet lacked much capability to communicate with each other or even to 'keep station' for naval warfare. More surprising, given the fact that ships had been sailing around the point of Brittany since pre-Roman times, this journey remained difficult in anything except favourable weather. Even then the western peninsulas of Brittany became choke-points where pirates or enemy ships could find rich pickings. Naturally enough, the security of this route linking England and Aquitaine was of major concern for English rulers.

Although the English attempted to patrol their own coasts and tried to stop French, Flemish and German ships from supplying enemy or dissident forces in Scotland, England as yet had nothing comparable to France's Clos des Galées in Rouen. Apart from a very small number of 'royal ships', the English crown had to hire vessels from private owners or temporarily 'arrest' them for military use as required. Most of the ships involved were of a type known as a 'cog' and their crews were still remarkably large, perhaps half as many as the number of troops being carried as passengers. Perhaps inevitably, the 'arrest' of ships and crews for military service led to many complaints from English ship-owners about the impact on trade. They also generally considered payment of three farthings a ton (thus according to the size of the ship) to be inadequate compensation.

On the other hand the ship-owners and crews of southern England seemed willing to take part in a little piracy – authorized or otherwise – as a source of additional income. Like Chaucer's Dartmouth Shipman, they were also extremely brutal, throwing most captives overboard:

Of nyce conscience took he no keep.
 If that he faught and hadde the hyer hond,
By water he sente hem home to every lond.[5]

The English fleet that attacked the Breton port of Saint-Malo in late March or early April 1373 probably included 'part-time pirates' as well as the 4,000 men-at-arms and archers commanded by the Count of Salisbury. They plundered seven fully laden Spanish merchant ships and pillaged the surrounding countryside, which prompted an uprising, as Froissart explained: 'The barons and knights of the country were much surprised at this, and declared that the Duke of Brittany (Jean IV) had sent for the English, they suspected him more than ever, and strengthened all their towns and castles in case of danger.'[6]

The French now invaded Brittany and found themselves widely welcomed. Duke Jean thereupon placed his family in the care of the English garrison at Auray and fled to England. Constable Du Guesclin was, in fact, still campaigning against remaining England-held outposts in Brittany when he was recalled to face a new threat. Before then he and the Duke of Bourbon attacked Jersey, off the coast of Brittany and Normandy, taking control of the castle and extracting a ransom from the island's inhabitants before leaving.

When Jean IV of Brittany arrived in England in spring 1373 with his remaining Breton supporters, he agreed to take part in the forthcoming

---

5 Translated as 'The nicer rules of conscience he ignored. If, when he fought, the enemy vessel sank, he sent his prisoners home; they walked the plank.' Coghill, N., *The Canterbury Tales*, London (1966), p.28
6 Froissart, John (Anon. ed. & tr.), *The Chronicles of England, France and Spain*, London (1906), pp.141–42

Duke Louis II of Bourbon rendering homage to King Charles V in 1371, shown in a 17th-century copy of a late 14th-century manuscript destroyed during a fire at the Chambres des Comtes in Paris. Each of the main figures is a simple portrait, identified by his heraldic cloak. (Bibliothèque Nationale, Ms. Fr. 20082, f.8, Paris)

campaign against France – but only in return for John of Gaunt handing over the Earldom of Richmond in northern England. This was agreed, but plans for the campaign were meanwhile changing. There was also notable diplomatic activity by both sides. For example, the Duke of Berry sent an ambassador to the Pope in Avignon with secret instructions, while the English government sent several embassies to Flanders in the hope of turning that region against King Charles of France. England was also fortunate in having a reasonably secure truce with Scotland, traditionally an ally of France, which was not due to end until 1384.

Coincidentally, the papacy chose 1373 to conduct a thorough investigation into the much criticized and now somewhat corrupt Crusading Order of Hospitallers (see Osprey Warrior 41: *Knight Hospitaller (2) 1306– 1565*). Its findings made dismal reading, with one of the most inefficient and corrupt regions being that of the Auvergne; soon to be the scene of the Great Chevauchée's epic winter march.

The French and English armies of the 1370s differed from those of the early part of the Hundred Years War in significant respects. Nevertheless, the *arrière-ban*, which summoned all those with a military obligation, was still widely used by Charles V. The French king still had direct control over only a small part of the realm, and even beyond this heartland around Paris his government was primarily concerned with the Seine valley, the Channel coast, Flanders, the frontier regions facing the Empire, and Burgundy. This was made clear by a royal ordnance of 8 November 1372 that dealt with local defence in these regions. Its emphasis was on castles, other fortifications and ensuring royal

One man works while the second has a drink, on a 14th-century carved wooden misericorde. During the Hundred Years War large numbers of ships were required to carry English armies to France. (*In situ* Cathedral, St David's, Wales)

control over the *châtelains* or governors of such places. Several of these would, of course, be targets of the Great Chevauchée, which was therefore a direct and specific challenge to the authority of the French crown. Elsewhere, local knights were generally selected for local responsibility in those regions facing English-ruled territory. This was most obviously in distant or rugged regions far from central government control, such as the Auvergne. Similarly it is worth noting that the armies with which the Duke of Anjou retook southern Aquitaine were recruited largely from the Languedoc region of southern France. Militarily, in fact, the kingdom of France was still very decentralized.

Nevertheless, stories 'from the front' clearly circulated across the country and may well have been used by the government to maintain support for the struggle against the English. One of the most touching was recorded in a treatise on domestic economy written some years after the Great Chevauchée by a distinctly unwarlike merchant for his young wife and generally known as *The Goodman of Paris*. One of its moral tales relates how 'By God, at Niort I saw an old dog, that lay upon the pit wherein his master had been buried, that had been slain by the English, and Monseigneur de Berry [the Duke of Berry] and a great number of lords were led there to see the marvel of this dog's loyalty and love, that day and night left not the pit, wherein was his master that the English had slain. And Monseigneur de Berry caused ten francs to be given to him, the which were delivered to a neighbour to find food for him all his life'.[7] This episode took place in July 1373 when the Duke visited Niort a few months after it had been retaken from the English by Bertrand du Guesclin.

Of more immediate impact upon the Great Chevauchée was the French focus on fixed defences. This period witnessed an increase in, and significant effort to modernize, not only castles but also the fortifications of church

---

7 Anon. (E. Power tr.), *The Goodman of Paris*, London (1992), p.73

The Great Seal of John of Gaunt, portraying him as King of Castile and León in Spain, as Duke of Aquitaine in France, as Earl of Derby, Lincoln and Leicester in England, and as Seneschal of England. (Public Records Office, London)

towers, bridges, monasteries and manor houses. There was also a notable increase in the power of fortified towns – the strategically important *bonnes villes* of France. Having been depopulated by waves of plague, they were now being repopulated by refugees from the war-ravaged countryside. Nor were all such refugees poor or desperate, but included wealthy members of the aristocracy who would play a major role in their military defence. Meanwhile, much of the French countryside largely escaped the problems described above and was now entering a period of economic revival. This in turn would finance the strengthening and modernization of the numerous *maisons fortes*, fortified manor houses of the minor nobility, though this was mostly seen after 1373.

Meanwhile, as a result of the French offensive, castles returned to their original function as a means of controlling the countryside, with King Charles V making sure that his castles were properly defended and manned. His brothers, the most powerful dukes of the realm, did the same within their own territories, as did lesser barons lower down the feudal order. In 1367 the French King ordered a new inventory of his fortified places, as a result of which those that could be made stronger were given priority while those deemed indefensible were destroyed. Charles V's edict also insisted that every lord and every town not only had to reinforce their ramparts but must ensure that these places contained adequate supplies, weaponry, munitions and defenders. Those who could not fulfil these demands were again obliged to demolish their defences.

From the mid-14th to the mid-15th century the typical French fortress was considerably heightened, with major towers no longer merely commanding their neighbouring walls. Almost every vantage point was soon being used as a platform where weapons could be based while the walls themselves were gradually provided with continuous machicolations. The results were certainly dramatic, though an increased use of more effective guns suddenly made these high walls a liability in the later 15th century. At the time of the Great Chevauchée, however, defence was going through a period of general superiority over offence, especially when facing armies like that headed by John of Gaunt, which had little in the way of siege artillery.

For Charles V and his senior commanders it remained vital that the enemy should not win control of any significant fortification, all of which seem to have been strongly garrisoned. This strategy proved very successful in 1373, obliging the English to march across a virtually deserted countryside, vainly trying to lure the French out of their fortresses. This the French only did when conditions were favourable, not hesitating to harass the enemy's rear, cutting off supplies and killing stray troops or stragglers.

It is therefore interesting to note that although the Great Chevauchée would attack several towns, the few places it did take were small and largely unfortified. Amongst those locations that were attacked, only Troyes and Sens would have really rated as *bonnes villes*. This name was given to urban centres identified by proper fortifications that rarely fell to English assault or siege during the Hundred Years War. Even more rarely did they suffer direct attack by English chevauchées, though enemy raiding seriously interrupted their trade.

Yet the defences of *bonnes villes* still had to be modernized, the newer features of the late 14th century including deeper and wider fosses or moats outside their walls, often with wooden palisades beyond. Charles V recognized the towns' importance as sources of wealth, as well as their potential as centres of discontent, so he worked hard to establish good relations with his *bonnes villes*. For their part the town or city authorities recognized the value of having effective fortifications. Though hugely expensive, these provided a secure centre for trade, manufacture and business, while proclaiming such security in a very public, highly visible manner. Hence the French king's repayment of one tenth of the cost of new or upgraded fortification in 1372 was a reflection of mutual interest as well as being a political bribe.

The problems caused by gangs of unemployed soldiers have already been mentioned, and their presence in some parts of mountainous central France probably influenced the direction taken by the Great Chevauchée. During the 1370s the Limousin area was particularly infested by these bands of freebooters, those of English origin or recent English employment still occupying many castles in the Viscomte and Bas-Limousin areas. From here their activities are known to have had a severe impact on the trade of small market towns such as Brive and Martel. The Auvergne region was similarly infested. In such areas freebooters continued the practice of forcing local inhabitants to pay a *patis*, a sort of protection money. Similarly, a rival armed gang could enforce an *appatisation*, a form of collective ransom extracted from those who had paid protection money to the 'wrong side'. English freebooters seem to have been particularly ruthless in destroying property and mutilating victims to ensure payment, while imprisonment for ransom rarely applied to captives of non-noble status, who either paid up or were killed.

It is, therefore, hardly surprising that much of the French peasantry of these regions had retreated into hills, where they lived in forests and caves. Similarly unsurprisingly, soldiers of all armies tended to be reluctant to penetrate such unknown areas unless they were themselves in sufficient numbers. This brutal and little-recorded aspect of the Hundred Years War often meant that French peasant rebels within English-ruled territory were unwittingly fighting for the French king, though they were not under French government control. One other feature that astonished raiders throughout France, and which again had some bearing on the course of the Great Chevauchée, was the speed and effectiveness of what might be called a 'bush telegraph' between villages, constantly forewarning those ahead of the approach of enemy forces.

THE PLAN

John of Gaunt's initial plan was for his army and fleet to assemble at Plymouth, then set sail on 10 May 1373 and land somewhere on the Norman or north Breton coasts. The army would then join forces with Duke Jean IV, who had not yet, of course, fled from Brittany. The allies would then presumably have struck southwards to relieve Aquitaine, or eastwards against the French capital of Paris.

Circumstances would force a major change, but until then recruitment proceeded along normal lines. In fact such enlistment was now somewhat different to what it had been at the start of the Hundred Years War. Feudal recruitment had changed, especially within England, where soldiers for armies serving outside the kingdom were now paid, professional mercenaries. For the lesser ranks the motives were economic and presumably a sense of adventure, plus a residual element of bullying by the government's 'commissions of array'.

Only amongst the aristocracy was there still some social, moral or political pressure to serve. The status of knighthood had, in fact, become a burden, both financial and because of the local government responsibilities it entailed. The number of traditional fighting knights or *strenui milites* had slumped even more dramatically, and it has been estimated that fewer than one in ten of a late 14th-century English army's men-at-arms were of knightly rank. The rest were squires or professional soldiers 'risen from the ranks' and wealthy enough to afford the very expensive arms, armour and horses required of such a role. Nevertheless there was still a sufficient pool of militarily professional knights, mostly the younger sons of the rural gentry, who provided an experienced 'officer corps' for armies such as that being assembled by John of Gaunt. Several such men are also known to have become specialists in various military fields, ranging from siege and naval warfare to chevauchées by wholly mounted and fast moving forces.

The size of units within English armies remained very irregular and there does not yet seem to have been the sort of attempt to impose some uniformity that was seen in late 14th-century France. Nevertheless, many units seem to have been balanced in the sense of including relatively regular proportions of men-at-arms and archers, especially mounted archers. A remarkable new database, using the abundant original documents available in English archives,[8] lists the names and ranks of 1,356 men who enlisted in 1373. In fact, these documents deal with more than one campaign: John of Gaunt's expedition to France, which continued into 1374; the 'Keeping of the Sea' under Sir Philip de Courtney, which had started in 1372; a standing force in Ireland under Sir Robert de Assheton, which also began in 1372; and a naval expedition under William de Montagu Earl of Salisbury in 1373. Of these, John of Gaunt's was the biggest, and the majority of the men enlisted for this campaign were described either as men-at-arms or as archers.

Other sources indicate that John of Gaunt enlisted 3,032 men-at-arms and 2,893 archers for his Great Chevauchée. The expedition thus had roughly equal proportions of men-at-arms and archers. Most other comparable English expeditions of this period were the same, though John of Gaunt's own expedition to France in 1369 was unusual in having almost twice as many archers as men-at-arms. John of Gaunt's own surviving archive also shows that around a quarter of the total force consisted of his personal retinue, though much of this was recently enlisted. The rest came from the retinues of 13 English and 15 non-English captains or commanders.

Senior ranks still tended to be drawn from the aristocracy while the commanders of the most important expeditions were usually members of the English royal family. For example, the Constable of the English army on the Great Chevauchée was Sir Edward Spencer, a patron of the famous chronicler Froissart, while the Marshals were Count Thomas of Warwick and Count William of Suffolk. In contrast, command of smaller forces or secondary theatres often went to professional 'captains'.

The remarkable speed of the 'bush telegraph' between villages has already been mentioned. What might seem even more surprising to modern readers was the speed and efficiency of the official 'posting system' in England, especially that between the Captain of Calais and London via Dover. The importance of this route was confirmed in 1372, when the government ordered various people along the route to supply official messengers with horses 'at reasonable prices'. These enabled such messengers to average 25 miles per day.

Westminster might have been as close as later medieval England had to a capital, but where the planning of the Great Chevauchée was concerned, John of Gaunt's Savoy Palace served as the nerve centre. Here his clerks and other servants of his household provided the administrative structure necessary even for a medieval army.[9] John of Gaunt spent more time there than anywhere else during the organization of the expedition, though he also travelled around the country a great deal. In addition to enlisting troops, purchasing huge numbers of horses and gathering supplies and ships, he also had to make provision for his own family. Thus the bureaucratic records include personal details, such as

8 Curry, A. (et al.), '1373', from *The Soldier in Later Medieval England* (2000), www.icmacentre.ac.uk/soldier/database/search_musterdb.phb

9 Armitage-Smith, S., *John of Gaunt's Register*, 2 vols, London (1911) passim

The *Décades de Tite-Live* was a mid-14th-century French translation by Pierre Bersuire of the Latin history by Livy (Titus Livius). A number of highly illustrated copies were made. This one dates from the reign of King Charles V and shows Roman protagonists in armour of the time of the Great Chevauchée, much as John of Gaunt and his men would have landed at Calais. (Bibliothèque Municipale, Ms. 730, Bordeaux)

arranging for coal and wood to be taken to Tutbury Castle in the Midlands, where his wife Constance would reside during his absence.[10] After the place of muster was changed from Plymouth to Kent, and as the date for departure approached, John of Gaunt established a headquarters at Northbourne, a grange of St Augustine's Abbey in Canterbury, which was conveniently located between the harbours of Sandwich and Dover.

However, John of Gaunt was also having financial problems. An expedition like the Great Chevauchée was extremely expensive, and he still owed considerable amounts of money from previous campaigns. In addition to the £15,762 he received from the government Exchequer, John of Gaunt took out several substantial loans, while his own network of castles and estates became centres for raising money and for assembling war supplies, military materiel and, of course, recruits. Men and materiel then had to be sent to the main mustering points and it is worth noting that individual archers were often given cash in advance to cover their travel expenses. During 1373 this tended to be around 40 shillings and, perhaps not surprisingly, John of Gaunt's correspondence reflects a concern that men might simply take the money and disappear.

One letter to an official named Robert Morton in Yorkshire stated: 'make sure that this is done and in such a way that they have no cause nor reason to excuse their non-appearance on the coast for default of payment', while he warned William Hornby, an official in Lancashire: 'And make sure that this is done and in such a manner that the expedition is in no way disrupted, understanding that if it is disrupted we would not wish to impute the blame to you in this case, and therefore do not neglect this, on account of the hazard involved, and as you wish to avoid upsetting us.'[11]

---

10 Goodman, A., *John of Gaunt: The Exercise of Princely Power in Fourteenth Century Europe*, London (1992), pp.52–53
11 Ibid., pp.222–23

Money was similarly a concern for those who were recruited. This is sometimes very clear in indenture documents: for example, one dated 16 March 1373 in which a squire named Robert de Haytfield clearly insisted upon his right to take and keep prisoners 'and other profits of war'. Of course, not all those who signed were soldiers; an indenture dated the previous day concerned a knight and his brother who was a physician surgeon named Brother William de Appilton. The latter was to be paid £40, and be allocated a gentleman clerk, a chamberlain, plus four horses with two boys to look after them.[12]

10 MAY 1373

Planned departure date from Plymouth

England was not one of the major centres of medieval art but it was famous for its alabaster carvings. These were exported across much of western Europe, usually in the form of portable religious images. Here a sleeping soldier forms part of a late 14th-century carving of Christ's Resurrection, which came from the Church of Saint-Michel in Bordeaux. (Musée d'Aquitaine, Bordeaux; author's photograph)

---

12 Armitage-Smith, S., *John of Gaunt's Register*, vol. I, pp.335–36

Loyalty or adherence to a particular captain tended to be more characteristic amongst squires and men-at-arms than amongst archers, yet most military units seem to have had a regional character with individuals preferring to serve beneath the banners of men from their own parts of the country. More surprising, perhaps, was the presence of Scotsmen in John of Gaunt's army. One such was John Swinton from the Scottish Borders, who served on condition that he was not expected to fight against his own country. In 1372 he was retained as an *esquire* with the higher than normal fee of £29. After returning from the Great Chevauchée, during which he served with distinction, he was again retained, this time as a knight with twice the fee. Clearly Swinton was a loyal follower of John of Gaunt; perhaps too much so, riding into London wearing his leader's badge at a time when John of Gaunt was highly unpopular. As a result he was dragged from his horse by an enraged crowd and saved only by the Mayor of London in person. Other less willing recruits included criminals seeking a royal pardon in return for military service. Even so, the resulting letters were not always accepted at face value and often had to be accompanied by proof that military service had actually been completed.

Then there was the question of horses, huge numbers of which were required and huge numbers of which tended to die if a campaign was extended into winter. This in turn often resulted in the need to compensate the animal's owner, which could prove very expensive when highly bred cavalry *destriers* were concerned. Normally, however, John of Gaunt's own clerks and local officials were expected to locate and purchase the necessary animals; the urgency of this requirement again being clear in surviving records.

Despite the Great Chevauchée's tendency to avoid sieges, John of Gaunt recruited military engineers and purchased the material they needed. This included bridging equipment and some siege weaponry. In April 1373 the 'receiver' of Tutbury was ordered to recruit four carpenters, two masons and two iron workers 'to make and work engines and trepgeutes and other special things needed by us for the same expedition'. Other such craftsmen were recruited in Lancashire and Leicestershire.[13] The Great Chevauchée similarly brought 'mobile', probably hand-operated, mills to grind wheat on campaign, in the correct assumption that the French would render their own inoperable before the English could capture them.

Finally there was the question of assembling or purchasing sufficient ships to carry the army to France. One such was a 'barge' or 'balinger' from London, a purpose-built fighting vessel powered by both sail and oars. England as yet possessed few such ships, but during the 1370s several towns and cities were asked to build them at their own expense for use in war by the crown. A surviving indenture, witnessed by John Piel the Mayor of London and other officials on 29 July 1373, provides an astonishing degree of detail about one such barge, its rigging and armament. Named the *Paul of London*, and with William Martlesham 'mariner of the aforementioned city' as its master, the vessel was to 'serve under the King'. Its equipment included

---

13 Goodman, A., *John of Gaunt*, pp.218–19; Armitage-Smith, S., *John of Gaunt's Register*, vol. II, pp.156–58

Philip the Bold, the first Duke of Burgundy to come from the Valois dynasty, was the chief opponent of the Great Chevauchée. This statue was carved by Claus Sluter, Duke Philip's own court sculptor. (*In situ* portal of the Charterhouse of Champol Church)

'1 pair of plates [full armour for the captain], 400 sheaves of arrows, with a tun [to store them in], 80 pavyz [large shields]' as well as '200 dartes, 30 launces [spears], 4000 quarels [crossbow bolts] for arblast [crossbow]'.[14] The city of York is also known to have built two ships for the crown, one named the *Peter* serving twice in 1373. Meanwhile the city of Bristol's promotion to the status of a county in 1373 was, according to its charter, 'in consideration of the good service given us (the King) in times past by their shipping'.

French planning in the face of the threatened English attack was, of course, dependent upon what French commanders knew, and when they knew it. According to the *Chronique du Bon Duc Loys* (Duke Louis II of

---

14 Riley, T.H., 'Delivery of a barge, provided by the City of London to serve under the King, together with the rigging and tackle thereof, to William Martlesham, its master (1373)', *De Re Militari website* (Feb 2009)

20 MAY 1373

John of Gaunt orders troops to gather at Dover and Sandwich

Bourbon), which was probably written in the 15th century, reports of a great English army preparing to invade France were first received after Christmas 1372. The army in question was also believed to be bigger than any that had come to France before. However, its target was thought – correctly at the time – to be somewhere on the western part of the Channel coast. The first known discussion of this threat seems to have been in March 1373, when Duke Philip the Bold of Burgundy made a short visit to Paris to meet his brother, King Charles V, before returning to Burgundy. Even at this early stage it seems that the cautious Charles V wanted to pursue a strategy of seeking to damage and weaken the enemy without exposing his own forces to unnecessary risk.

Quite when French troops began to assemble in and around the city of Tours is unclear, but this was certainly under way by the late spring and early summer of 1373. Philip the Bold came to inspect his own Burgundians in this concentration, which also included siege weaponry. Although an army at Tours was in the right place to resist an attack via Brittany or even Normandy, it was wrongly positioned to face an assault in the north, via Picardy. However, the French still had enemies to face elsewhere, and early in July some of Philip the Bold's Burgundians were sent from Tours to support the Duke of Berry in Aquitaine. Similarly Bertrand du Guesclin spent most of July and much of August, after the invasion had started, fighting against other English forces in Brittany. Whereas Du Guesclin eventually made truces in Brittany and for a while joined the struggle against John of Gaunt, French vigilance in the south-west never seems to have relaxed.

Here, on 28 April 1373, Duke Jean of Berry had been instructed by his brother the king to retain an additional 300 men-at-arms to protect newly

Communications in medieval France and England were better than is generally recognized, at least where government messenger systems were concerned. Here, in the *Décades de Tite-Live* manuscript, which was made within a few years of the Great Chevauchée, a ruler either receives or sends two official messengers. They are identified by spears and the *scrips*, or decorated pouches attached to their belts. (Bibliothèque Municipale, Ms. 730, Bordeaux)

reconquered territory in Guyenne. During the late spring and early summer the Duke of Berry accelerated such recruitment, and amongst the 178 knights and 603 squires known to be serving under his command were very senior men such as Hugues de Froideville the Marshal of the Auvergne, Jean la Personne the Vicomte of Aunay, and Alain de Beaumont the Senechal of Poitou who had already been given command of the castle of Sainte-Néomaye, which he himself had recaptured from the English.

Other men under the Duke of Berry's banner had only recently transferred their allegiance from the English to the French crowns. On the other hand surviving documents hint at problems of slackness and lack of discipline amongst some of the Duke of Berry's officers. The Duke was also clearly impatient for the arrival of several pieces of artillery sent by the King to help in Poitou but which were held up at Tours. Meanwhile several senior figures in the Order of Hospitallers had already accepted responsibility for defending the Auvergne and Velay regions against roving bands of Anglo-Gascon *routiers*. One such was Béraud de Dienne from Cantal in the Massif Central. Born around 1333, he was the Hospitaller Commander at Celles before 1360, and was soon captain of the town of Saint-Flour. In 1369 he had a small force of two brother knights, 17 brother sergeants and some non-Hospitaller knights. In 1373, the year that the Great Chevauchée appeared in his area, Béraud de Dienne was at the head of Sarlat, Celles and their dependencies, these being the two most important Hospitaller Commanderies in the Haute Auvergne.

The lack of evidence for French preparations in Burgundy might suggest that the Great Chevauchée's daring invasion of that part of the country came as a surprise. Given the Burgundian nobility's renowned pride and fear of dishonour, Duke Philip the Bold's ability to stop his knights

12 JUNE 1373

John of Gaunt made Lieutenant of the Realm of France

As always in medieval warfare, it was the rural peasantry who suffered most from the depredations of the Great Chevauchée. Those shown in this mid-14th-century window might have been based upon English shepherds, but their French cousins would have looked much the same. ('Annunciation to the Shepherds', English stained-glass window, Victoria & Albert Museum, inv. 2270-1900, London)

attacking the Great Chevauchée at every opportunity says a lot for his power of command. Perhaps it to some extent reflected the clear and continuing efforts at reform that characterized the French military system following the disasters of the first part of the Hundred Years War. Although the revised duties and powers of the Constable were only written down in January 1381, this probably reflected changes which might have been under way in 1373. According to the new rules the Constable of France had the right to command all men in battle – except, of course, for the King – from the highest nobles to the common soldiers. He was senior to the Marshal, who could not order the formations without the Constable's consent. He was also in command of all battles, chevauchées, and so on, though he must give up his place to the King if he was present. The Constable was also in command of all spies and scouts, yet he was obliged to explain all his expenditures to the royal clerks.[15]

At a lower level, this period saw French men-at-arms increasingly divided into regular formations of ten men known as *chambres*. One recorded example was the *chambre* of the knight Jacques de Harcourt, which consisted of himself, three other knights and six squires. The 'free companies', which were still causing problems in various parts of France, similarly provided the French crown and great barons with troops and ready-made military formations. Nevertheless they required close control and supervision, as shown in one of King Charles V's charters dated 17 October 1373. This was one of several attempts to insist that each 'captain' only have the types and numbers of troops agreed in his contract or indenture. Less than three weeks after John of Gaunt's Great Chevauchée finally staggered into Bordeaux, Charles V issued another ordnance, insisting that captains should not enrol men with insufficient equipment and who were prone to pillage, but only those fully equipped and who behaved properly. The need to repeat such instructions several times clearly shows how difficult it was to have them obeyed.

The official French communications system was comparable to that of England's, and was similarly faster and more reliable in some areas than in others. For example, the role of the fortified town of Chalon-sur-Saône as a major hub of long-distance communication and for the exchange of official correspondence probably contributed much to the success of French resistance to the Great Chevauchée. Written evidence for this communications system is nevertheless sparse. However, one document from the Clos des Galées in Rouen, written at Harfleur and dated 17 August 1373, was an order from a certain Jehan Cornevalois concerning payments for the 'Armée de la Mer' or fleet, mostly for messengers who had already carried letters to various important people as part of preparations against the English threat.[16] The distances covered by Duke Philip the Bold of Burgundy during his preparations and on campaign against the Great Chevauchée – every night's stop being known – show

15 Cosneau, E., *Le Connétable De Richemont (Artur de Bretagne) (1393–1458)*, Paris (1886), pp.504–05
16 Chazelas, A., *Documents Relatifs au Clos de Galées de Rouen et aux Armées de Mer du Roi de France de 1293 à 1418, vol. 1*, Paris (1977–78), pp.156–57

that travel, though difficult by modern standards, was no hindrance to a senior military commander in late 14th-century France.

John of Gaunt's change of plan was made official on 20 May, when the men and ships preparing to assemble at Plymouth were told to gather at Dover and Sandwich instead. The collapse of support for Duke Jean IV in Brittany probably made this inevitable, yet it undoubtedly delayed the start and rendered the success of the expedition doubtful. Its ultimate objective also seems to have been clouded. Was it now to be simply a great raiding expedition, causing as much economic and political damage to the heartland of the French monarchy as possible? Might it hope to attack Paris if circumstances seemed favourable? Or did John of Gaunt always hope to march all the way to Bordeaux and retrieve the English position in Aquitaine? If so, what route did he initially have in mind, since the ultimate decision to cross the highlands of the Auvergne in early winter still seems astonishing if not downright desperate? Unfortunately the original sources do not provide a clear answer, and it is possible that both John of Gaunt and Jean of Brittany always intended to keep their options open.

Once inside enemy territory it was normal for late medieval armies to expect to live off the land and such booty as they could gather. This was well suited to the ravaging and devastation tactics of a chevauchée, as long as the army did not destroy so many crops that it starved itself! On the other hand, this style of warfare encouraged military attitudes that some commentators already found distasteful. For example Geoffroi de Charny, in his *Book of Chivalry*, included a section on 'Those Who are Brave But Too Eager for Plunder'. His concern, however, stemmed mainly from the lack of discipline and control that this could cause within an army. 'It often happens that on the entry into a town won by force, those who are so greedy for plunder dash hither and thither and find themselves separated from those of their companions who have no thought for gain but only for completing their military undertaking. And it often happens that such men, who ride after and hunt for great booty, are killed in the process . . ., that which is thought to be already won can be lost again and lives or reputations as well.'[17]

Around 15 years after the disappointments of the Great Chevauchée, an English Dominican friar named Bromyard was particularly critical of such behaviour: 'Yet nowadays, alas, princes and knights and soldiers go to war in a different spirit; with their cruel actions and desire for gain, they incline themselves more to the ways of the devil than to those of God; for they set out for war not with prayers, but rather with oaths and curses in their mouths; nor do they fight at the expense of the king or of themselves, but at that of the Church and of the poor, despoiling both.'[18]

Not surprisingly the French, who tended to be on the receiving end of this form of warfare, were similarly critical. In 1387, in his *Tree of Battles*, the French cleric Honoré Bonet prayed: 'May it please God to put into the

---

17 De Charny, Geoffroi (R.W. Kaeuper & E. Kennedy ed. & tr.), *The Book of Chivalry of Geoffroi de Charny: Text, Context and Transliteration*, Philadelphia (1996), p.99
18 Allmand, C.T., *Society at War: The Experience of England and France during the Hundred Years War*, Woodbridge (1998), p.39

Today Dover is the main ferry-port linking England with France and it was equally important during the Middle Ages. It was here, and in nearby Sandwich, that John of Gaunt ordered his army to assemble in 1373, ready to be carried to Calais. (Author's photograph.)

hearts of Kings to command that in all wars poor labourers should be left secure and in peace, for in these days all wars are directly against the poor labouring people and against their goods and chattels. I do not call that war, but it seems to be pillage and robbery. Further, that way of warfare does not follow the ordinances of worthy chivalry or of the ancient custom of noble warriors who upheld justice, the widow, the orphan and the poor.'[19]

Brutal reality made such targeting of civilians almost inevitable and the Great Chevauchée would be no exception. Nevertheless, some types of countryside were clearly more vulnerable than others, and were therefore more likely to be targeted. Arable land could soon be resown and was rarely abandoned whereas orchards and vineyards took much longer to re-establish. It also seems that it was easier to re-establish small-scale peasant holdings than it was to rebuild larger aristocratic estates, which tended to require substantially greater investment in mills and other forms of infrastructure. The latter, of course, inevitably provided tempting targets for enemy raiders. All this would mean that the fertile rolling hills and valleys of northern and north-eastern France would suffer greatly from John of Gaunt's forthcoming expedition, whereas the higher and bleaker lands of the Massif Central offered the increasingly desperate invaders less to destroy and less to eat.

Quite when the French learned of John of Gaunt's change of plan remains a mystery, though on 10 July Duke Philip of Burgundy was warned to install garrisons in some strategic northern positions. It was soon clear that Philip the Bold would be in charge of French resistance and it cannot have been long before he realized that the enemy would attack from Calais. By late July the Duke of Burgundy had established his HQ at Amiens and on the 29th of that month he sent final warnings of the impending English assault to the

JULY 1373

English troops shipped to Calais

19 Allmand, C.T., *Society at War*, p.40

Duke of Bourbon, to Constable Du Guesclin, and to frontline garrisons at Crotoy and Aire-sur-la-Lys.

By then a squadron of five galleys and a *lin* or small communications ship, commanded by a member of the Genoese Grimaldi family, were cruising in the lower Channel as allies of France. They stocked up with food and supplies at Harfleur in August, which suggests that they were too late, or more likely too few in number, to have been able to challenge the carrying of John of Gaunt's army to France. Nevertheless, Philip the Bold and his army were not the only ones in a position to challenge the forthcoming Great Chevauchée. According to the *Chronique du Bon Duc Loys*, King Charles V, his other brothers and various senior commanders had installed forces in Troyes in June 1373. Others were, or soon would be, summoned from the south, including Jean de Vienne, described as a 'brave and dashing captain both ashore and afloat'.

Even since Calais and its immediate vicinity had fallen to the English in 1347, the French had been strengthening the surrounding region, not just with castles and fortified towns, but with fortified churches and abbeys. Together these formed a network that local garrisons and military units could use as outposts or observation points. Very few of them could, nevertheless, hope to withstand a major assault, nor could the system as a whole contain a significant invasion launched from Calais.

This area may have been commanded by Jean de Semp, a famous soldier from a leading Artois family whose exploits against the English would be celebrated in a ballad by Eustache Deschamps, written at the time of his death in 1386. De Semp was certainly Captain of Picardy in 1369–70, and again in 1372. He then served as Captain-General in the Limousin in 1374, but was back as Captain-General of Picardy in 1375 and 1379–80. However, the Captain-General of Picardy in 1373 might have been Hue de Châtillon,

29 JULY 1373

The Duke of Burgundy warns of the imminent English assault

Few cities have endured such a war-torn history as Amiens in northern France and yet retained a picturesque charm. The Duke of Burgundy established his headquarters here in July 1373, and the two columns of the Great Chevauchée passed perilously close the following month. (Author's photograph)

a knight from Champagne or Picardy, who had been captain of the region between the rivers Oise and Lys and the coast in 1372. After suffering several setbacks, he would be replaced by Guichard Dauphin, the Master of Crossbowmen, in 1379. The situation was clearer in Laon, where Jean III de Bueil, a nobleman from the Tours region, had been appointed captain by King Charles V in 1373. His role against the Great Chevauchée would be celebrated in several sources, including Froissart's famous chronicles.

Other leading French soldiers who now made their way to Amiens included the Duke of Lorraine, Jean d'Artois the Count of Eu and the Count of Saint-Pol, who were greeted by the Duke of Burgundy on 16 July. Like the English, the French also employed foreign volunteers, or perhaps more accurately exiled allies, one of whom was a Welsh prince, Owain Lawgoch. He spent many years in French service and had already taken part in a naval raid against Guernsey in 1372. Owain Lawgoch was now placed at the head of 100 men-at-arms under the command of the Duke of Burgundy, having been retained to keep watch on the Great Chevauchée.

Most of the middle-ranking commanders were, of course, Frenchmen and surviving documents showed that they were retained with military retinues of various sizes. These ranged from Renaud VI de Pons, a nobleman from the Saintonge who had previously fought for, rather than against, the Black Prince in Spain. Renaud changed sides several times and was now retained at the head of 30 men-at-arms. In contrast Guillaume de Mareuil, a knight from the Angoulême region, was retained in 1373 with just ten men-at-arms to shadow and harass the Great Chevauchée. He must have done well because a few years later he was retained at the head of 30 men-at-arms and was appointed Senechal of his home territory of Angoulême in 1383.[20]

---

20 Contamine, P., *Guerre, État et Societé à la Fin du Moyen Âge: Études sur les Armées des Rois de France 1337–1494*, Paris (1972), pp.562–91

THE RAID

The English parts of John of Gaunt's army were shipped from Sandwich and Dover to Calais during July 1373, along with Jean of Brittany's retinue. Precisely when John of Gaunt himself joined them is unclear as he was still at Northbourne, supervising operations and dealing with his affairs in England during most of that month. He had to appoint new constables to be in charge of his English castles because most of his existing adherents would take part in the Great Chevauchée. Tutbury Castle in Staffordshire had meanwhile been made ready for John of Gaunt's family and he had written his own will.

John of Gaunt now wielded great authority, having been appointed by his father Edward III as Commander-in-Chief of the King's forces, as Lieutenant of Aquitaine and as Lieutenant of the Realm of France. The latter might sound like a nominal position, reflecting the English ruler's revived claim to the throne of France, but in fact it gave John of Gaunt almost complete authority on campaign in territory 'reconquered' even temporarily as his army marched across France. These titles and authority were officially 'commissioned' in a document dated 12 June. That same month 'Prayers for King John (nominally of the Spanish kingdom of León and Castile) in his Expedition of Arms' were offered in churches across the land.

Unfortunately, the chroniclers who recorded the shipping of the army to France had little apparent interest in the non-aristocratic details of naval matters. On the other hand, the early English *Morte Arthure*, an archaic version of the *Tales of King Arthur and his Knights of the Round Table*, does contain a remarkable description of such an operation. It has even been suggested that the *Morte Arthure* was written a few years later as a criticism of Edward III's warlike policy in France. In this fictional version, the organized chaos of an army as it embarked was described with extraordinary accuracy. Sergeants-of-arms were instructed to 'arrest' ships and assemble a fleet at Sandwich. Here sheriffs assigned quarters to lords, their retinues and to common soldiers. Meanwhile other men load barges, which in the 14th century were warships rather than mere floating containers, with the military equipment the army would need:

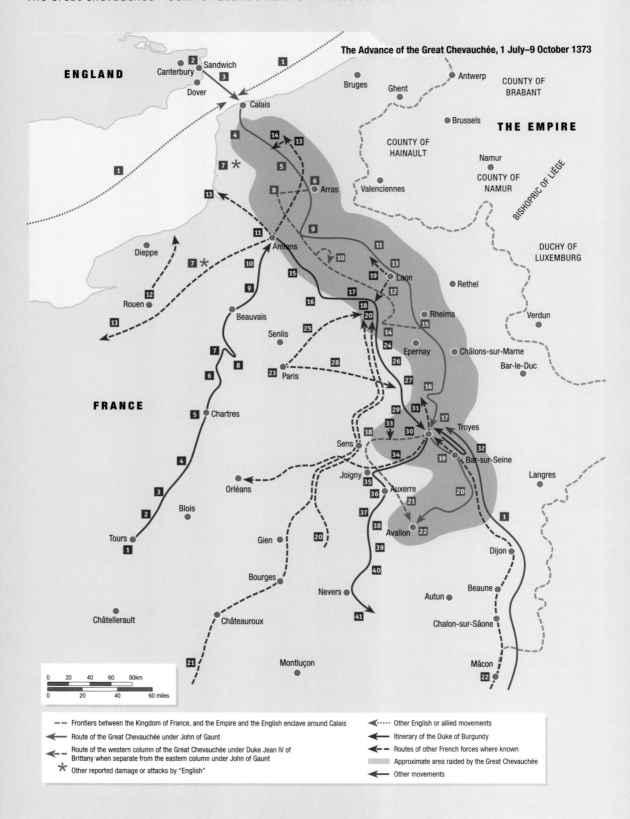

The Great Chevauchée – John of Gaunt's Raid on France 1373

ENGLAND

Canterbury · Sandwich · Dover · Calais

The Advance of the Great Chevauchée, 1 July–9 October 1373

Bruges · Ghent · Antwerp · **COUNTY OF BRABANT**

Brussels · **THE EMPIRE**

COUNTY OF HAINAULT

Namur · **COUNTY OF NAMUR** · **BISHOPRIC OF LIÈGE**

Valenciennes

Arras

Dieppe

Amiens

Laon · Rethel · **DUCHY OF LUXEMBURG**

Rheims · Verdun

Rouen · Beauvais

Senlis · Epernay · Châlons-sur-Marne · Bar-le-Duc

Paris · Troyes

FRANCE

Chartres · Sens · Bar-sur-Seine · Langres

Orléans · Joigny · Auxerre

Blois · Avallon · Dijon

Tours · Gien · Beaune

Bourges · Nevers · Autun · Chalon-sur-Sâone

Châtellerault · Châteauroux

Montluçon · Mâcon

Scale: 0 20 40 60 80km / 0 20 40 60 miles

Legend:

- – – – Frontiers between the Kingdom of France, and the Empire and the English enclave around Calais
- ◄——— Route of the Great Chevauchée under John of Gaunt
- ◄– – Route of the western column of the Great Chevauchée under Duke Jean IV of Brittany when separate from the eastern column under John of Gaunt
- ✱ Other reported damage or attacks by "English"
- ◄········ Other English or allied movements
- ◄——— Itinerary of the Duke of Burgundy
- ◄–·– Routes of other French forces where known
- ▨ Approximate area raided by the Great Chevauchée
- ◄——— Other movements

36

THE ADVANCE OF THE GREAT CHEVAUCHÉE, 1 JULY–9 OCTOBER 1373

■ Key to English and allied movements

1 Additional troops from Brittany, Hainault and Germany join John of Gaunt's main force in Calais
2 John of Gaunt at Northbourne Grange outside Sandwich (6 July)
3 John of Gaunt sails to Calais (July)
4 Great Chevauchée marches out of Calais arrayed in 'three battles' (4 August), ravages the Abbey of Licques and camps on 'hills of Helfaut' during the second night of its march (5 August)
5 Great Chevauchée, still arrayed in 'three battles', passes Thérouanne and makes camp 15–20km beyond (6 August)
6 Great Chevauchée reaches Arras where John of Gaunt and Jean of Brittany lodge for two nights in the Abbey of Saint-Eloi (7–8 August); the army then divides into two columns, the eastern commanded by John of Gaunt and the western by Jean of Brittany
7 Elements from the Great Chevauchée reportedly active near Montreuil; Sainte-Geneviève-en-Caux subsequently requested tax exemption because of damage inflicted by the 'English' in 1373 (probably a transcription error for villages called Saint-Geneviève in the Aisne or Oise regions)
8 Western column makes unsuccessful assault on Doullens, then crosses the river Aire
9 The two columns of the Great Chevauchée combine near Bray, which they unsuccessfully attack, then cross the river Somme between Bray and Corbie, separate and attack Cappy (19–20 August)
10 Western column occupies and ravages the town of Roye (21–28 August) but is unable to take the strongly defended church, also makes an unsuccessful assault on the castle of Nesle; Duke Jean IV of Brittany sends a formal defiance to his previous sovereign, King Charles V of France
11 Eastern column crosses the river Oise near Ribemont where one of its units is defeated by French troops including elements from Laon (around 22–23 August)
12 Western column establishes camp between Pont l'Evêque and Vailly (around 23–25 August)
13 Eastern column makes camp near Crécy-sur-Serre (7–8 September)
14 Detachment from western column commanded by Gautier Hewit defeated by French forces under Jean de Vienne, Jean de Bueil and Robert de Béthune at Oulchy-le-Château (9 September)
15 Two columns probably join forces to cross the Marne south-west of Rheims
16 Elements of the Great Chevauchée make half-hearted assault on Plancy but are driven off by the Duke of Bourbon in a skirmish known as the *Barrières Amoureuses* (19 September)
17 Great Chevauchée reaches Troyes (21 September), attacks the suburbs but is driven off by Olivier de Clisson and the Duke of Bourbon (25 September); Great Chevauchée leaves Troyes (26 September)
18 Western column heads west towards Sens (26 September) but falls into a double ambush by De Clisson, suffering the worst battlefield defeat of the campaign (probably 27 September)
19 Eastern column continues south-east and crosses the Seine at Gyé
20 Eastern column ravages Pothières
21 Western column, no longer raiding but keeping together as a defensive formation, rejoins eastern column in the Avallon area (first week of October)
22 Great Chevauchée reported ravaging the Avallon area (by 10 October)

■ Key to other participants and events

1 The Cardinal Archbishop of Ravenna and the Cardinal Bishop of Carpentras travel to Troyes from the Papal Court at Avignon and unsuccessfully attempt to mediate peace negotiations

■ Key to French movements

1 Duke of Burgundy at Tours to inspect Burgundian troops amongst French forces assembled to face a feared English invasion of Brittany (1–3 July); some troops sent from Tours to support the Duke of Berry in Poitou (early July)
2 Duke of Burgundy, probably accompanied by most of the troops from Tours, reaches Château-Renault (4 July)
3 Duke of Burgundy reaches Vendôme (5 July)
4 Duke of Burgundy reaches Châteaudun (6 July)
5 Duke of Burgundy reaches Chartres (7 July)
6 Duke of Burgundy reaches Houdan (8 July)
7 Duke of Burgundy reaches and stops at Mantes where he is instructed by Charles V to garrison strategic locations to face an English threat from Calais (9–10 July)
8 Duke of Burgundy goes to Neauphle to see his step-grandmother, Queen Blanche (11 July); the troops with him would probably have gone direct from Mantes to Beauvais
9 Duke of Burgundy reaches Beauvais (12 July)
10 Duke of Burgundy reaches Conty (13 July)
11 Duke of Burgundy reaches and establishes HQ at Amiens (14 July–16 August)
12 The Clos de Galées in Rouen is ordered to send munitions, including artillery, to the castle of Longueville-sur-Scie to face a feared English assault on Dieppe (27 July)
13 Duke of Burgundy sends messages to troops in Brest (Brittany), Crotoy and Aire-sur-la-Lys to warn of imminent English assault
14 Count of Saint-Pol harries the Great Chevauchée as it passes Aire-sur-la-Lys
15 Duke of Burgundy moves to Montdidier (17 August)
16 Duke of Burgundy establishes new HQ at Compiègne (18–20 August)
17 Duke of Burgundy moves to Ambleny (21 August)
18 Duke of Burgundy establishes new HQ at Soissons (22 August–9 September)
19 Jean de Bueil the Captain of Laon takes a force to Ribemont and helps defeat an element of the Great Chevauchée (around 22–23 August)
20 Louis the Marshal of Sancerre, Jean de Bueil the Captain of Laon, and other commanders join forces with the Duke of Burgundy at Soissons (around 25 August)
21 Duke of Anjou, bringing forces from the south, joins the main French concentration (first week of September)
22 The Seneschal of Beaucaire and Nimes brings forces from Languedoc to join the Duke of Anjou in Troyes (first week of September)
23 French leaders hold strategy meeting in Paris, including Charles V, the Duke of Alençon, the Duke of Bourbon, Olivier de Clisson and probably Bertrand du Guesclin, but probably not the Duke of Anjou and certainly not the Duke of Burgundy (10 September); De Clisson, probably the Duke of Bourbon and Du Guesclin leave Paris to join main French army (11 September)
24 Duke of Burgundy at Château Thierry (10 September)
25 Du Guesclin and the Duke of Bourbon harrass the Great Chevauchée in the Vermandois region (from 11 September); Duke of Bourbon then joins the main French army assembling at Troyes (by 19 September); Du Guesclin returns to Brittany to continue the campaign there
26 Duke of Burgundy at Montmirail (11 September)
27 Duke of Burgundy at Sezanne (12–13 September)
28 De Clisson joins forces with the Duke of Burgundy at Sezanne (13 September), then continues to Troyes
29 Duke of Burgundy at Saint-Just-Sauvage (14 September)
30 Duke of Burgundy establishes new HQ at Troyes (15–19 September)
31 Duke of Bourbon takes a unit to defend Plancy and defeats an element of the Great Chevauchée at the *Barrières Amoureuses* (19 September)
32 Duke of Burgundy visits his two-months-pregnant wife at Jully-sur-Sarce (20 September), then returns to Troyes to supervise operations against the Great Chevauchée (21–26 September)
33 The Captain of Marigny-le-Châtel attacks elements of the Great Chevauchée (probably 26 or 27 September)
34 King Charles V in Troyes orders senior commanders to return to the Brittany, Poitou and Limousin fronts (final days of September)
35 Duke of Burgundy at Joigny (27 September)
36 Duke of Burgundy establishes new HQ at Auxerre (28–30 September)
37 Duke of Burgundy at unidentified 'castle of Beache' (1 October)
38 Duke of Burgundy at Druyes-les-Belles-Fontaines (2 October)
39 Duke of Burgundy at Varzy (3 October)
40 Duke of Burgundy at Premery (4–6 October)
41 Duke of Burgundy at Decize (7–9 October)

Bryngez blonkez [horses] on bourde, and burlyche [tall] helmets;
Trussez in tristly [confidently load] trappyde stedes,
Tentez, and othire toylez [equipment], and targez [shields] fulle ryche,
Cabanes [cabins], and clathe-sekkes, and coferez [chests] fulle noble,
Hukes [riding-horses], and haknays [pack horses], and horses of armes.[21]

Within Calais the arrival of such a large army must have caused problems for the existing English administration. Those in command of the frontier were Nicolles Cannoie at Guines and Jehans de Harleston at Ardres, while the role of a man described by Froissart as the Sire de Goummegnies is unclear. Behind them a considerable army had now gathered. Despite the availability of numerous original documents, its true size remains unknown. Again according to Froissart, the army consisted of 3,000 men-at-arms, 6,000 archers and 2,000 'other men'. Froissart's preoccupation with deeds of chivalry by individual members of the knightly class caused him to list those he considered important, and they included representatives of many of England's noble families, as well as others from further afield plus 'many other good knights who are too many to mention'.

The English and Breton contingents were now joined by several hundred mercenaries or volunteers from Hainault and Brabant in what is now Belgium, from Germany and perhaps by additional dissident elements from Brittany. John of Gaunt's own high standing also encouraged about 300 Scottish 'lances' to join him on the forthcoming adventure. According to the *Grandes Chroniques de France*, John of Gaunt and his main ally, Duke Jean of Brittany, spent some time in Calais and its marches or frontier before setting off, presumably refining their plans or making last-minute adjustments to the army's organization and array. Clearly there was no realistic hope of launching a surprise attack, and given John of Gaunt's subsequent efforts to bring the main French army to battle he probably did not want to do so.

Having arrayed their forces outside Calais, the Anglo-Breton commanders marched along the old road up the hills to Guines and Ardres, the low-lying marshland crossed by the modern main road being undrained in the 14th century. They crossed the frontier into French territory on the morning of Wednesday 4 August, marching in three *battles* or main formations, in close order, with the vanguard fully ready for combat, banners flying, trumpets blaring and drums beating. The three *battles* were, in fact, entirely traditional, consisting of a *vanward* (vanguard), *mainward* (centre) and *rearward* (rearguard), while the van and flanks were further protected by smaller units of men-at-arms and mounted archers. The Marshals, the Earls of Warwick and Suffolk, were in command of the *vanward*. John of Gaunt and the Duke of Brittany commanded the *mainward* with the veteran and highly experienced Sir Hugues (Hugh) of Calverly. This veteran campaigner now served as what would now be called a 'chief of staff'. Next came the vital transport and baggage train, while the *rearward* was commanded by the Constable, Lord Despencer.

---

21 Barnie, J., *War in Medieval Society: Social Values and the Hundred Years War*, London (1974), pp.147–48

After ignoring the small castle of Montoire (now Nielles-lès-Ardres) where a knight of Picardy named Houdecourte guarded the frontier, discipline was strictly maintained as it was unclear how the French would react. Nevertheless the invaders almost immediately set about spreading havoc as far as they could. The destruction of the Abbey of Licques may have been carried out during the army's first-night stop in the vicinity, or it may have been done by a detached unit. According to Froissart: 'They advanced at the rate of about three leagues a day, and at night quartered together, keeping a strict and strong watch to prevent surprise', one league being approximately the same as 5km.

The Great Chevauchée now headed for Saint-Omer, which was held by the Viscount of Meux with a substantial force of men-at-arms. A barrage of arrows and crossbow bolts drove off a mounted company of English and Scottish troops who approached the *barrières* or outer defences but there is no evidence that the invaders actually attempted to take the town.

This late 14th-century English manuscript is mainly of interest because it includes a very early representation of a cannon being used during a siege. However, the wooden fence in front of the town gate is probably a simplified illustration of the *barrières*, which were intended to stop a surprise enemy attack from reaching the main defences. (British Library, Ms. Cotton Nero, E.II, pt. p.1)

THE STAND-OFF AT MONT-SAINT-ELOI

7–8 AUGUST 1373

KEY

- ▪▪▪▪ English marching in three *batailles* plus baggage
- ○ English encampment
- —— English column, arrayed for *chevauchée*
- → English movements
- ○ French in defensive position
- ⸦⸧ Presumed French observation position on Roman road

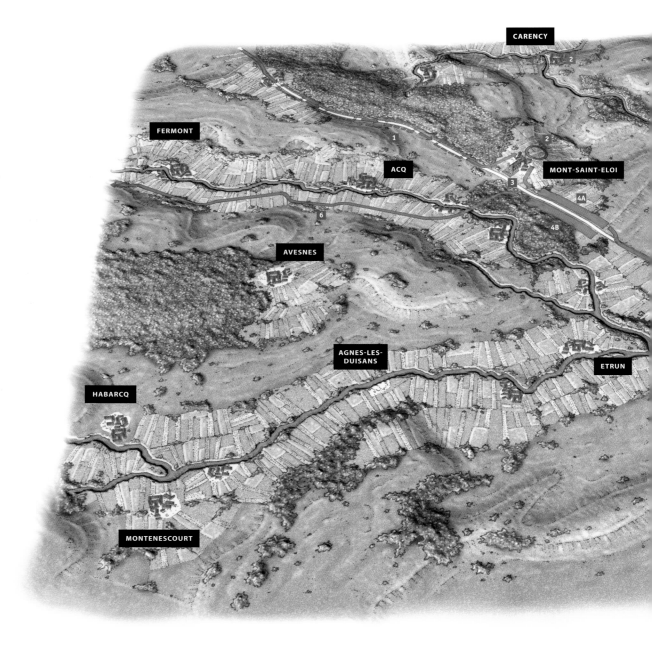

CARENCY

FERMONT

ACQ

MONT-SAINT-ELOI

AVESNES

AGNES-LES-DUISANS

ETRUN

HABARCQ

MONTENESCOURT

ENGLISH POSITIONS AND MOVEMENTS 1 – 6

1   The English army approaches from Calais (7 August). During the medieval period the line of the ancient Roman road, which is believed to have gone straight across the wooded hills, had been abandoned and the road instead went through the village of Camblain-l'Abbé. The English army was still in the three batailles (*vanward*, *mainward*, then baggage train and *rearward*) that had been adoped outside Calais.

2   The English make camp on the hill at Mont-Saint-Eloi (7–8 August).

3   John of Gaunt, Duke Jean of Brittany & their immediate entourages establish themselves in the Abbey. Whether or not the army created a defensive position is unrecorded.

4   The English army is reorganized into two large columns (9 August), under John of Gaunt (A) and Jean of Brittany (B). The bridging equipment & the available siege weaponry probably accompanied John of Gaunt.

5   John of Gaunt's column continues along the old Roman road but does not attack Arras, instead marching around the fortified city, probably on the west side, and continues towards Bray.

6   Jean of Brittany's column heads westward in the direction of Saint-Pol.

FRENCH POSITIONS AND MOVEMENTS 1 – 4

1   Arras was strongly garrisonned and had its own militia, probably receiving instructions from the Duke of Burgundy 60km away in Amiens.

2   The 13th century castle at Carency was certainly in use during the 14th century and is likely to have contained a small French garrison, probably under orders from the Count of Saint-Pol 50km away at Aire-sur-la-Lys.

3   The French garrison at Arras most likely established an observation position some way up the Roman road, to keep watch on the English and report on their activities.

4   Any French observation position in this area would have withdrawn within the fortifications of Arras when John of Gaunt's column approached on 9 August.

SAINT-VAAST

ARRAS

John of Gaunt established his second night's camp a few kilometres to the south, on a wooded plateau outside the village of Helfaut, between Saint-Omer and the similarly fortified town of Thérouanne. The latter had a garrison that reportedly included 200 men-at-arms led by the seigneurs of Sempy, Brimeaux and Poix supported by Lionel d'Airaines. The invaders are unlikely to have considered it too strong to be attacked and probably decided not to be slowed down by unnecessary sieges or to risk direct assaults, especially as there was a substantial French force at Aire-sur-la-Lys only 10km to the east. In fact Froissart maintained that the Count of Saint-Pol, based in Aire, harried the English and 'caused them great damage'. He also claimed that both sides 'communicated with each other very courteously', which was how this chivalric chronicler expected his knightly heroes to behave.

Thérouanne stood at a junction in the old Roman road system and from here the straight line of one such route led south-eastwards, directly towards Arras. About 8km from Arras, the invading army halted and made camp next to the Abbey of Mont-Saint-Eloi, on a low hill on the northern side of the Roman road and overlooking the plain towards Arras. John of Gaunt and Duke Jean naturally made their quarters within the abbey. Whether the damage caused in 1373, and mentioned in papal archives, was done at this point or when the frustrated invaders moved off a few days later is again unknown.

John of Gaunt may have regarded this as a potentially good defensive position and have hoped the French would attack, as they had done so disastrously at the battles of Crécy in 1346 and Poitiers in 1356. Certainly his army stayed put for two nights, but the French had altered their tactics since the early part of the Hundred Years War and the Duke of Burgundy, in charge of the defence of northern France, showed no sign of accepting a formal challenge. It was almost certainly at this point that John of Gaunt and Jean of Brittany changed their plans. What might originally have been intended as a full-scale invasion now became a Great Raid – the *Great Chevauchée* of contemporary sources.

This necessitated a fundamental reorganization of their forces, which, by the time they set out again on 9 August, consisted of two virtually autonomous armies. It was an array designed to ravage and devastate as wide an area as possible, though still probably with the hope of bringing the main French army to battle.

While what was now the left-hand column under John of Gaunt marched on past Arras, what was now the right-hand column under Duke Jean of Brittany turned sharply west. Its precise route is unknown, either going past Saint-Pol towards Hesdin or veering towards Doullens. Demonstrations were made against both, though neither was taken. Strategically this could indicate that the Great Chevauchée was trying to threaten Amiens, where the Duke of Burgundy had his HQ, from the north-west and north-east. Still the French commander would not rise to the bait.

The *Grandes Chroniques de France* does not always make a clear distinction between these two columns. Yet the events it describes mostly

This well-known late 14th-century manuscript illustration showing soldiers pillaging and clearly getting drunk appears in most books about the horrors of medieval warfare. But for the people who lived in the path of the Great Chevauchée it was a current reality. (*Chroniques de France*, British Library, Ms. Roy. 20.C.VII, f.41v, London)

seem to concern the western under the Duke of Brittany, stating that the enemy headed for Hesdin where they remained several days in the *parc* or open area outside the main gate, without attacking the town or its castle. The same was reported at Doullens, after which Jean of Brittany's army marched via Beauquesne towards Corbie on the river Somme. Meanwhile some of the Duke of Brittany's raiders might have been active even further west, close to Montreuil. Perhaps these movements by Jean of Brittany and John of Gaunt, north and east of Amiens, were still part of an effort to get the Duke of Burgundy to make a rash counter-attack. If so they failed, for Philip the Bold belied his nickname and remained with the bulk of his army in strongly fortified Amiens, where he had established his HQ back in mid-July. Nor would he make his move until 17 August, when he cautiously headed south-eastwards to Montdidier, by which time both columns of the Great Chevauchée were heading south-east towards the river Somme, deeper into the Kingdom of France. From then on he shadowed the raiders, usually from a distance of around 20km, and remained between them and Paris. Only when the threat to the French capital had passed did the Duke of Burgundy attempt anything more risky.

Respected early 20th-century English historian of these events S. Armitage-Smith seems to have misunderstood or even to have misrepresented the Duke of Burgundy's actions during this period, writing that 'The Duke was playing his own game. His predecessor in 1360 had bribed Edward III not to ravage Burgundy, and had left the Regent (his elder brother and future King Charles V) and the rest of France to their fate. With equal preoccupation for the safety of his own lands the Duke showed now plainly enough his anxiety to get to the south. He left Amiens on August 17; the English did not reach Braye till the 20th.'[22] In fact the Duke of Burgundy showed great restraint, controlled his more hot-headed captains and followed a cautious plan that would subsequently be confirmed by a council of senior French commanders in Paris.

---

22 Armitage-Smith, S., *John of Gaunt*, London (1904), pp.108–09

4 AUGUST 1373

Anglo-Breton force crosses into French territory

Nevertheless the price a large part of France would pay for this cautious, if ultimately successful, strategy would be high. Modern research has shown that a large medieval army was capable of devastating and pillaging a swathe of territory 25km from its line of march, thus creating a zone of destruction 50km wide. The work of pillaging, like that of foraging, was usually left to *valets* and *pillars*, the personal servants of knights and other camp-followers, who were usually of peasant origin. Such 'dirty work' was considered demeaning for a knight. It could also be very dangerous, the pillagers inevitably being hated by the peasantry and usually being killed if caught at a disadvantage. So the *pillars* would work in packs, focusing their attention on mills, crops and herds during the Great Chevauchée.

The invaders suffered their first significant check when they reached the river Somme. Having failed to get a response from the Duke of Burgundy, the two columns of the Great Chevauchée came together again near Bray-sur-Somme. This they reportedly besieged but were unable to take, despite having at least some siege weaponry. Once again it seems more likely that the attack was to neutralize any threat to their own crossing of the Somme between Bray and Corbie. Yet it was clearly a real fight and Froissart was particularly impressed by the fact that some local clerics took part.

Once south of the river Somme the two forces sacked the large nearby village of Cappy on 19 or 20 August. Naturally enough, reports of these events and of the enemy's movements were sent to French commanders. One was written by the Captain of the castle of Nesle, a few kilometres north-east of Roye, who sent a courier to the authorities in Reims on 20 August, warning that the English were now at Bray and Cappy. From Reims the message was hurriedly forwarded to Troyes, which had been designated as the main assembly point for French armies.

The following day the English and their allies seized the town of Roye, though apparently they were unable to take the main church into which the

Like so much of northern France, Roye has suffered from frequent invasions. The town was sacked by the Great Chevauchée for seven days, though the attackers were unable to take the strongly defended Church of Saint-Pierre. This fine 13th-century edifice with 15th- and 16th-century additions was, however, damaged during a German air raid in 1940. (Author's photograph)

The Great Chevauchée suffered a number of minor setbacks before part of one of its columns was emphatically defeated outside Oulchy-le-Château. Although it was not enough to make the English and their allies retreat, it probably convinced them not to strike at the French capital of Paris. (Author's photograph)

French garrison had retreated. The invaders remained in occupation of Roye for a week, during which Duke Jean of Brittany finally wrote his formal defiance to Charles V, renouncing his homage and recognizing King Edward III as sovereign ruler of France. The English also attacked the castle of Nesle and during the course of this somewhat half-hearted assault Guyon Grassin from Poitiers, a spy in John of Gaunt's service, was either captured or went over to the French garrison. The information he provided was probably useful at the time, but has come down through the chronicles in a rather garbled form.

The Great Chevauchée now set about their work of devastation with enthusiasm, wreaking havoc across what Froissart described as the 'fair and rich land of Vermandois'. Roye, Essigni, Vendeuil and Rémigny were burned to the ground. The destruction was so thorough that for several years the French King's exchequer abandoned any hope of extracting the usual tax revenues from these towns. In fact a document dated 4 January 1374 recorded that Charles V ordered their taxes be remitted.

Once again the early English version of *Morte Arthure* offers a remarkable description of the devastation and misery caused by a chevauchée:

> Walles he welte downe [overturned], wondyn knyghtez,
> Towrres he turnes, and turmentez the pople,
> Wroghte [made] wedewes [widows] fulle wlonke [proud], wrotherayle [miserable] sygnes,
> Ofte wery [lament] and wepe, and wryngene theire handis;
> And alle he wastys with werre, thare he awaye rydez,
> Thaire welthes and theire wonnynges [dwellings], wandrethe [sorrow] he wroghte.[23]

Now that John of Gaunt seemed more concerned with devastating the Vermandois than with threatening Paris, the Duke of Burgundy moved ahead of the Great Chevauchée's anticipated line of march and established a new HQ at Soissons. There he would remain from 22 August until 9 September. Meanwhile he maintained frequent correspondence with Louis the Marshal of Sancerre, Jean de Bueil the Captain of Laon and various other commanders,

19–20 AUGUST 1373

Cappy sacked

23 Barnie, J., *War in Medieval Society*, p.149

most of whom brought their troops to Soissons on 25 August. That same day the governor of Reims received another report that a substantial body of enemy troops had crossed the river Oise and made camp between Pont l'Evêque and Vailly. In response a formidable French force was assembled around Soissons to watch, harass and if necessary confront the Great Chevauchée.

As yet the invasion was of little immediate concern to other French commanders in the south. The Duke of Berry was still campaigning in Poitou, but the Duke of Anjou did send a contingent of 2,000 men-at-arms and 500 crossbowmen from the Languedoc region. Commanded by the Senechal of Beaucaire, they arrived in time for some of them to take part in a battle outside Oulchy-le-Château on 9 September. The Duke of Anjou himself was summoned to Paris by King Charles V and therefore had to abandon a minor campaign in the Bigorre region of the central Pyrenees where he had been besieging Mauvezin and Lourdes.

The Constable of France, Bertrand du Guesclin, left the campaign in Brittany but went directly to the Vermandois area rather than stopping in Paris. There his retinue was involved in shadowing the English during the first week of September where Du Guesclin apparently campaigned alongside Duke Louis of Bourbon. Yet this was a very brief involvement, as the Constable was back in Paris within a few days and then promptly returned to Brittany later in September to continue his siege of English-held Brest.

Meanwhile the Great Chevauchée suffered a minor but embarrassing setback near Ribemont on the south bank of the river Oise. Here the retinue of Sir Hugues of Calverly, a highly respected English captain, was badly cut up though Calverly himself escaped blame, being with John of Gaunt at the time. Nevertheless, this skirmish boosted French morale. It seems that the French captain, Guillaume des Bordes, had arrived in Saint-Quentin and found there the Sire de Bousies. The latter was on his way home from Hainault to Ribemont, to help guard the castle where his wife, a daughter of the lord of nearby Chin, was living. Although Guillaume des Bordes could lend him only ten crossbowmen, De Bousies pressed ahead while Sir Guillaume hurriedly called for volunteers and eventually set out for Ribemont with some 40 men-at-arms and 30 mounted crossbowmen. About two leagues (approx. 10km) down the road they found Jean de Bueil, the Captain of Laon, encamped with his troops.

The entire countryside was infested with enemy raiders but learning that a substantial English force had passed Ribemont early that day, the two commanders agreed to help the Sire de Bousies. After riding a further half a league the French came in sight of Sir Hugues of Calverly's men. By attacking immediately they caught the 80 or so English by surprise, capturing much of their equipment or baggage, which they then took across the river Oise into the castle of Ribemont. Here they found the lord of Chin, who had arrived from a different direction with 60 men-at-arms. In fact a substantial French force was now assembling at Ribemont, many knights, squires and their retainers having come from up and down the Oise valley to fight the English.

Having been told by observers on the walls that another *routte* or unit of devastators consisting of '100 helmets and four pennons' was approaching, the

French decided to form up in battle array outside Ribemont. Rather than waiting to be attacked, however, the English promptly lowered their lances and charged, bursting through the French ranks and stirring up considerable dust. With their battle cry of 'Notre-Dame de Ribemont' the French counter-attacked, with the Lord of Chin's banner leading the way. Froissart again captured the spirit of the age: 'So began a battle of about 200 men, strong and hard fought with many good feats of arms on both sides. The lord of Chin who was called Sir Gilles fought with a heavy mace on the bascinets [helmets] of the English that they fell to the ground. Finally the French won the ground and the English lost many killed or captured. Very few escaped. The knights and squires re-entered Ribemont where they put their prisoners. It was about the hour of Vespers. The following morning they departed for Laon.'[24]

Froissart's famous chronicles survive in more than one version and one of them adds further details. For example, the Lord of Chin received such a powerful blow to his helmet that he would have fallen from his horse had his squire not helped him. In fact Gilles de Chin suffered from this blow for the rest of his life. On the English side confusion was also caused by the fact that the coat-of-arms of Chin were almost identical to those of the Lord of Coucy, who was regarded as a friend of England. Amongst the prisoners were two brothers named Pembroke, one a knight and the other a squire, who were taken by the Sire de Bousies. Froissart also maintained that the English could still have besieged Ribemont, but chose not to do so because they were in a hurry to press on.[25]

On 10 September, a few days after the clash at Ribemont, King Charles V and some of his senior commanders met to agree a strategy. This Great Council would determine the rest of the campaign and those present were the Dukes of Alençon, Bourbon and possibly Anjou. The Duke of Burgundy was meanwhile at Château Thierry in command of the field army, while the Duke of Berry was still in Poitou. Also there were the Breton veterans Bertrand du Guesclin and Olivier de Clisson. Although the French position was much stronger than it had been in earlier decades, strengthening the hands of those in favour of a major confrontation, De Clisson argued in favour of restraint. He was supported by Du Guesclin and Bourbon and, perhaps not surprisingly, this was what the cautious King Charles eventually decided. Whether the words that Froissart put into the mouths of the king's council were ever spoken is immaterial, as they certainly summed up the strategy that Charles V now adopted: '*Laissez-les-aller. Par fumières ne peuvent-ils venir a votre héritage; il leur ennuira, et iront tous à neant*' (Let them pass.

Olivier de Clisson was junior to the Constable of France, Bertrand du Guesclin, in 1373, though he would himself become Constable after Du Guesclin's death. Both men were fearsomely effective Breton commanders and Clisson became known as 'The Butcher'. (Effigy of Olivier de Clisson, *in situ* church of Notre-Dame-du-Ronvier, Josselin; M.C.E. Jones' photograph)

24 Froissart, Jean (G.T. Diller ed.), *Chroniques, Livre 1, Le Manuscrit d'Amiens*, Geneva (1993), pp.281–82
25 Froissart, Jean, 'Chronicles', various extracts translated by J. Dunbabin, S. Muhlberger, J. Bourcher & H. Nicholson, *De Re Militari website* (Feb 2009)

Most fighting during the Great Chevauchée seems to have been on foot and there were no major battles, just a series of skirmishes, ambushes and generally unsuccessful assaults upon small towns or suburbs. Judging by the shapes of their shields, the men on the left in this illustration from the *Décades de Tite-Live* are dismounted knights, while those on the right seem to be infantrymen. (Bibliothèque Municipale, Ms. 730, Bordeaux)

With smoke they cannot deprive you of your heritage; they will tire and they will come to nothing).

The Council then broke up with an agreement to assemble all available forces at Troyes in Champagne, except for Du Guesclin, who would continue the campaign in Brittany. Far away in Poitou the Duke of Berry now fell ill, and although the sickness was not fatal it was serious enough for him to summon an 'experimental' doctor from La Rochelle who arrived at the patient's bedside on 20 September. By then a great deal had happened in the north.

John of Gaunt is known to have been at Crécy-sur-Serre, just north of Laon, and at Mons-le-Château on 7 and 8 September. For whatever reason, the Great Chevauchée no longer seemed to threaten Paris but was bent on causing as much damage as possible as it made its way towards the Champagne area of north-eastern France. Skirting the strongly fortified and garrisoned hilltop city of Laon, the English were nevertheless given strict orders not to damage the lands of Coucy. Enguerrand VII, the current Lord of Coucy, was actually fighting as a mercenary in northern Italy, and, being Duke of Bedford in England as well as a leading French baron, had, in the words of Froissart, 'not interfered with the wars in France' since fighting for King Jean II at the disastrous battle of Poitiers.

On its right flank the Great Chevauchée now had a steadily increasing French army under the Duke of Burgundy; on its left flank, in the town of Laon, was a garrison of about 300 French and Breton men-at-arms, plus an unknown number of crossbowmen. For their part, the two separate columns of the chevauchée took care to remain in touch while continuing to burn and slaughter wherever they could. Although the English and French usually just watched each other carefully, the raiders were challenged several times. John of Gaunt and Jean of Brittany converged to cross the river Aisne at Vailly-sur-Aisne but then apparently separated once again, probably at Braine, to increase the area of devastation.

21 AUGUST 1373

Roye captured

Watermills were prime targets for the Great Chevauchée. If there was a watermill here at Courmononcle, near Troyes, in the 14th century, it would undoubtedly have been destroyed because the Great Chevauchée went right past its door. (Author's photograph)

The moated castle of Vault-de-Lugny is now a high-class hotel, but at the end of September 1373 raiders from the Great Chevauchée were ravaging the surrounding countryside. (Author's photograph)

The next major clash was another setback for the invaders, this time for the western column under Duke Jean of Brittany. It took place outside Oulchy-le-Château: a fortified village with a rather old-fashioned 12th–13th century castle, which had, at that time, yet to be modernized. Oulchy was not apparently a very important location; however the results of what was little more than a skirmish again had a profound impact upon French morale, and perhaps on that of the invaders as well. The defeated English commander, Gautier Hewit, was regarded as one of the most experienced men and he appears to have been on a reconnaissance rather than raiding when caught by a superior French force at dawn on 9 September. The details are again supplied by Froissart, who was clearly fascinated by small-scale conflicts, especially where the actions of individuals were seen and recalled by participants on both sides.

Gautier Hewit with his mounted force of 50 men-at-arms and 20 archers had made camp outside the seemingly harmless fortifications of Oulchy. But these walls hid about 120 men-at-arms who had apparently assembled quietly, perhaps during the night. What is clear is that, around dawn, Jean de Vienne,

9 SEPTEMBER 1373

Battle outside Oulchy-le-Château

John of Gaunt's great raid clearly brought bridging equipment with it, and for a while this enabled the army to ignore broken bridges. Here a late 14th-century French manuscript illustration shows an army using a bridge of boats. (*Chroniques de France*, British Library, Ms. Roy. 20.C.VII, f.136b, London)

Jean de Bueil the Captain of Laon, Robert de Béthune and the Viscount of Meux attacked so suddenly that Gautier Hewit did not have time to put on his complete armour. He mounted his horse 'without his plates' but with his shield on his shoulder and his lance in his hand, then joined the fight. A French knight named Jehans del Mans, 'strong and valiant' and perhaps more importantly fully armoured and strongly mounted, spurred against Gautier Hewit, piercing his body with his sword. When the English saw Gautier fall from his horse 'wounded to death' they were disheartened. Furthermore, the French assault had been so sudden that Hewit's flag was not yet fully unfurled. This was important in a medieval battle because the flag provided a rallying point in case of defeat. As a result the French took many prisoners and 'departed without damage' while John of Gaunt and other English lords were 'greatly saddened' by the death of Gautier Hewit.[26]

The *Grandes Chroniques de France* added that Jean de Vienne captured ten senior knights and 23 squires – the fate of the English archers not being mentioned in any source. On the other hand the presence of the Senechal of Beaucaire and Nîmes in this small battle was highly significant, indicating that reinforcements sent by the Duke of Anjou from southern France had not only arrived but were already active.

The Great Chevauchée did not attack Rheims where John of Gaunt's father, King Edward III, had failed 13 years earlier. Instead the two columns of raiders sacked the surrounding area before heading towards the river Marne and the Champagne region. Meanwhile the Duke of Burgundy, having received two heralds who informed him of the 'discomfiture' of the enemy outside Oulchy, continued to shadow his enemies from the west. On 13 September he joined forces with De Clisson at Sezanne. King Charles and his officials meanwhile continued to recruit troops. During September they are known to have got agreement from the higher aristocracy and many of *bonnes*

---

26 Froissart, Jean (G.T. Diller ed.), *Chroniques*, pp.285–86

villes to raise forces or get financial contributions; the local authorities of Arras and Saint-Quentin sending crossbowmen 'within France, against the enemies of the kingdom' now that the threat to their own cities had passed.

The river Marne was the biggest such obstacle that the English had yet faced, especially as the main bridge had been destroyed. Nevertheless, the presence of military engineers and craftsmen in the army, and the availability of abundant timber in that area, meant that the river was crossed safely. The Great Chevauchée now passed close to Châlons-sur-Marne but did not attack, which suggests either that the invaders were now in some difficulty or that they were unaware of the parlous state of the town. In fact Châlons-sur-Marne had been almost bankrupted by the need to build new fortifications and had then suffered a major flood in January 1373 that destroyed most of its houses.

Instead the raiders passed west of Châlons and, in the words of Froissart, 'The Duke and his troops ravaged the town of Vertus and in front of Epernay ransomed the lives of all they found there, great pillage along the fine river Marne'. Papal records confirm that the Abbey of Vertus was 'troubled by the English' in 1373. It was now harvest and time to gather the vintage of this famous wine-producing region, but for the peasantry a year's worth of hard work went for nothing as they sought refuge within any fortified place that seemed strong enough to resist the raiders.

On the French side, the Duke of Burgundy seems to have been finding it difficult to stop his men from rushing out to defend the people, villages and fields, yet he stuck grimly to the King's orders. Meanwhile French troops and their leaders were assembling in and around Troyes, which the Duke of Burgundy and Olivier de Clisson reached on 15 September. They were only a few days ahead of the enemy. Some sources claim that the Duke of Burgundy now frittered away 12 days, playing tennis and *dès*, a board game using dice. He supposedly lost many games to Jean d'Artois the Comte of Eu and some of the other commanders who joined him in Troyes. Amongst them were Gui de la Trémoille, the Count of Ligny and the Constable Du Guesclin who arrived between 20 and 27 September. The Duke of Anjou was also there.

In reality the Duke of Burgundy seems to have been organizing his forces, which, for the first time on this campaign, now represented the greater part of the strength of France. He also had urgent family matters to consider and on 20 September made a hurried visit to Jully-sur-Sarce to see his wife, who was two months pregnant. He also wanted news of his other children, who were at Rouvre and Talent, their security being shared among the Captain of Dijon with three companies of nine knights, Guy de Cicons with four companies of nine knights, and an urban militia of between 60 and 80 men.

The Duke of Burgundy returned to Troyes the following day to supervise operations. By then events were moving fast. He gave responsibility for day-to-day military matters to his Marshal, Guy de Pontailler, who was allocated 1,200 men-at-arms to protect Troyes and its surroundings. These troops skirmished with the Great Chevauchée several times, but one minor clash caught the attention of chroniclers. It took place at Plancy-l'Abbé, about 30km north of Troyes, and came to be known as the *Barrières Amoureuses*. On 19 September, two days before the English arrived, the Captain of Plancy

OVERLEAF
An English reconnaissance unit of 50 men-at-arms and 20 mounted archers commanded by Gautier Hewit, one of the most experienced English veterans, made camp outside Oulchy-le-Château on 8 September. However, Hewit was unaware that the garrison of Oulchy was being substantially strengthened and at dawn the following morning the English camp was surprised by a larger French force. Its 120 men-at-arms were led by Jean de Vienne, Jean de Bueil and Robert de Béthune. Hewit himself did not have time to put on his plate armour before rushing into the fight, though he did carry his shield and lance. The English commander was then attacked by a French knight, Jehan del Mans, who struck Hewit a mortal thrusting blow with his sword. The English lost ten knights and 23 squires captured, only a few of the reconnaissance unit escaping.

sought a meeting with the Duke of Bourbon. His name was Jehan de Nedonchel and he requested 50 men-at-arms, promising them a fine adventure as the enemy crossed the river Aube near his castle of Plancy. Not only did the Duke of Bourbon agree, but he decided to come along as well. He selected the best men in his *hôtel* or retinue, including Jehan de Chastelmorand, who carried the Duke's banner, his brother the Sire de l'Espinasse, the Sire de Montaigut, the Sire de Chaugny his chamberlain, Himbert de Couture, Bertrandon Ernaud, a man named Baulsurre and another called the Borgne (squint-eyed) of Veaulce. They went to Plancy and awaited the enemy.

When the English appeared, the French arrayed themselves in front of the gate, in what was described as 'the finest *barrière* which could be seen', and watched as the English passed by. It apparently took the Great Chevauchée two days to do so, and all this while the Frenchmen remained fully armed outside the wooden *barrière*. When too many English came against them they pulled back behind the *barrière*, at which point the enemy attacked. The resulting fight seems to have been with spears between dismounted men across the *barrière*, almost like a particularly ruthless tournament. When those inside saw an advantage, they charged out, fought hard then fell back within the *barrière*. Both sides lost several men killed or wounded, one of those on the French side being Bertrandon Ernaud. He was struck by an arrow 'below the breast' and suffered a long time, which indicates that archers also took part at least on the English side. After nightfall the English retreated, or perhaps more correctly continued their march to Troyes, which they reached on 21 September.

As on previous occasions, the Great Chevauchée now ravaged the surrounding area while the French refused to be drawn. An embassy also arrived from the papal court in Avignon. It was headed by the Archbishop of Ravenna and the Bishop of Carpentras, both of whom were cardinals. They now attempted to negotiate with John of Gaunt and with King Charles

The dating of the simple wall-paintings in the castle of Saint-Floret in the Auvergne remain a matter of debate. They illustrate scenes from the epic tales of King Arthur's Knights of the Round Table. This region was relatively poor and isolated, so its defenders may well have been equipped in this old-fashioned style. (Author's photograph)

V, who was now himself in Troyes. Both received the cardinals politely but neither was prepared to offer meaningful concessions.

Once it became clear that nothing could be achieved by talking, John of Gaunt drew up his forces and issued a formal challenge. Charles still refused, so the English and their Breton allies crossed the undefended moat and entered the suburbs of Troyes. Suddenly, the French emerged from the fortified main city and drove the invaders out with considerable loss. Whether this was really an ambush, as some historians have suggested, or was simply a vigorous counter-attack by 2,000 men-at-arms is unclear. Nevertheless, the French claimed 600 enemy killed and around 400 taken prisoner. Amongst these captives was an English captain named Jehan Bulle (John Bull) and three Bretons, who were beheaded as traitors. Others claims were more conservative, suggesting 120 killed and 180 captured. More particularly, the Hospital of Saint-Esprit in the suburbs of Troyes was apparently burned down by the Great Chevauchée in 1373 and was for many years unable to help the poor of the area.

That night the English retreated to a new position between 2 and 3km from Troyes. The following day they broke camp and moved off in two separate directions. This appears to have caused some uncertainty in the French command, but King Charles ordered detachments to shadow both, one unit of 100 men-at-arms following Jean of Brittany's column towards Sens. If the French were not sure what would happen next, John of Gaunt is believed to have now made the decision that most observers think doomed the Great Chevauchée to near-disaster.

Like all later historians, Armitage-Smith had the great benefit of hindsight when he wrote that John of Gaunt 'now stood at the parting of the ways: the advance from Calais to Troyes had produced no engagements and no military result. He could go back, which would be inglorious, or he could go on, which would be useless. So much was clear, for the tactics of the enemy had paralyzed the English attack. But the general failed utterly to realize the altered condition under which he had now to conduct the campaign . . . The Duke could not have peace with honour. He chose honour with disaster, and went on.'[27]

John of Gaunt now led his column further up the north-east bank of the Seine, eventually crossing the river at Gyé. Meanwhile Duke Jean crossed the river just downstream from Troyes and led his column towards Sens. It was probably the latter march which the French Captain of Marigny-le-Châtel attacked with his garrison on 26 or 27 September, though without doing much damage. The Great Chevauchée was now in an area where frontiers between the territories that formed part of King Charles V's own feudal domains and those forming part of the Duchy of Burgundy were exceptionally complicated. In the late 14th and early 15th centuries Marigny-le-Châtel was, for example, one of several fiefs held by Bernard de Chateauvillain, and under such circumstances it was clearly impractical for major seigneurial lords like the Duke of Burgundy to limit their actions to the defence of their own estates.

According to the *Chronique du Bon Duc Loys*, the western column soon established itself in the suburbs of Sens, but there is no evidence of Duke

---

27 Armitage-Smith, S., *John of Gaunt*, pp.109–11

JEAN DE MONTFORT, THE DUKE OF BRITTANY FALLS INTO A DOUBLE AMBUSH LAID BY OLIVIER DE CLISSON NEAR SENS

27 SEPTEMBER 1373

KEY

▭ English position in suburbs of Sens

▬ English force in pursuit of supposed French scouts

⇢ English movements

▭ French garrisons

▬ French in ambush positions

→ French movements

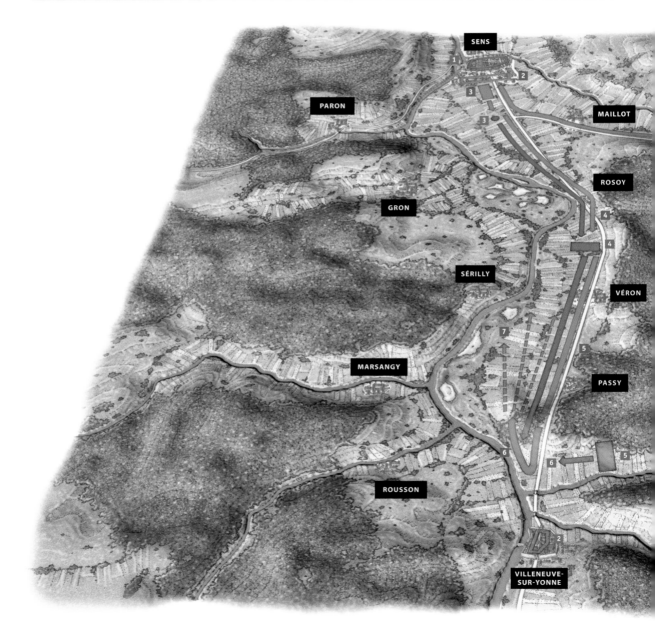

ENGLISH POSITIONS AND MOVEMENTS

1 The western column of the Great Chevauchée under Duke Jean of Brittany approaches Sens from Troyes, along the valley of the river Vanne.

2 Jean of Brittany and his troops take control of the suburbs of Sens.

3 A substantial English force pursues a supposed French scouting party.

4 The English in pursuit of the "scouts" apparently defeat a first French ambush.

5 The pursuing English lose cohesion.

6 The pursuing English are attacked & defeated by a second or main French ambush.

7 English fugitives flee back towards Sens.

FRENCH POSITIONS AND MOVEMENTS

1 French garrison in Sens.

2 Almost certainly a French garrison in Villeneuve-sur-Yonne.

3 A small French force of apparent "scouts" observe the English outside Sens but retreat when attacked.

4 The first French ambush, probably between Rosoy and Véron, attacks the pursuing English but then retreats.

5 The second or main French ambush under Olivier de Clisson is probably positioned in the valley of the river Sainte-Ange.

6 The main French ambush attacks and defeats the English pursuers, taking many prisoners.

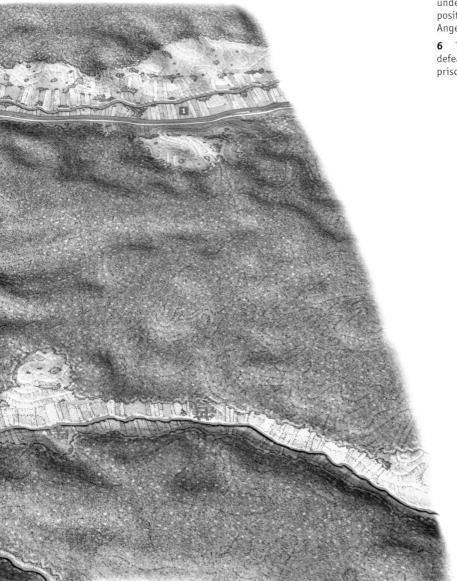

Jean of Brittany attacking the main fortified town. Instead he, or a substantial part of his army, was lured into an elaborate ambush. The Duke of Burgundy was still in operational command of French forces in this region and he is known to have left Troyes on 26 September. He spent the following night at Joigny, then the nights of 28 to 30 September at Auxerre. Olivier de Clisson and his men may have been with the Duke of Burgundy, or may already have been operating as a separate unit between Auxerre and Sens.

It seems most likely that on 27 September De Clisson was in command of around 1,500 men, both his own followers and some of the Duke of Burgundy's retinue. An ambush, reportedly consisting of 1,200 men-at-arms under De Clisson himself, was located 'two leagues' (approximately 10km) from Sens and was probably somewhere near the small but fortified town of Villeneuve-sur-Yonne, roughly midway between the Duke of Burgundy's current position at Joigny and the town of Sens. A forward ambush of 200 men-at-arms was established 'one league' away, midway between Sens and the main ambush, probably near or between the villages of Véron or Rosoy. De Clisson now sent a small unit to observe the English outside Sens and lure them into the ambush. This they did with complete success, being pursued by a substantial number of enemy horsemen as far as the first ambush. This then retreated, at which point the pursuers' discipline seemingly failed and, according to the *Chronique du Bon Duc Loys*, the English now charged 'recklessly and in disarray' – only to be hit by De Clisson's much larger main ambush. As a result around 600 English and Bretons were killed and many others taken prisoner.[28]

King Charles V's decision to send some of his senior commanders back to Brittany, Poitou and Limousin had probably been taken the previous day, 26 September. De Clisson now seems to have rejoined the Duke of Burgundy's main army. Meanwhile Duke Jean of Brittany cannot have intended to continue westward on his own while his ally, John of Gaunt, was campaigning in an almost diametrically opposite direction. They must surely have intended to rejoin forces at some point, so his march southwards, past the scene of his recent discomfiture, is likely to have been pre-planned. John of Gaunt's column, if not that of Jean of Brittany, was still enthusiastically devastating everything it could reach. However, the summer was now ending. The harsh terrain of the Massif Central might still lie some way ahead, but autumn approached, which meant that it would become increasingly difficult for the Great Chevauchée to live off the land.

Having crossed the Seine at Gyé, the eastern column under John of Gaunt ravaged Pothières near Châtillon-sur-Seine before heading west to link up with the western column. Together the invaders now had a final fling in the beautiful countryside around Avallon. One small and touching detail that somehow survived in the records of bigger events was the fact that the raiders stole the chalice and various other religious ornaments from the church in the village of Magny, close to Avallon. By now orders had been sent to all French local authorities in the area, instructing them to collect provisions and

---

28 Chazaud, A-M., *La Chronique du Bon Duc Loys de Bourbon*, Paris (1876), pp.54–55

remove the working iron parts from mills, to deny them to the enemy. A letter sent by the *bailli* of Auxerre to the wife of the Duke of Burgundy on 1 October reported the presence of raiders at Isle-sous-Montrèal, at Sainte-Colombe, close to Pontaubert, and at Vault-de-Lugny.

Meanwhile the Duke himself was still shadowing the Great Chevauchée, moving from Joigny to Auxerre, Varzy, Premery and Decize in a line-of-march parallel to the John of Gaunt's route. Isolated detachments were attacked where possible, as happened at Brion near Joigny. On the other hand the Hospitaller Commanderie of Pontaubert between Vault-de-Lugny and Avallon was so badly damaged that the Duke of Burgundy subsequently gave a large sum of money to its commander, Guillaume de Fontenay, to restore the place.

From this point onwards it becomes more difficult to identify the Great Chevauchée's route with much precision. However, it is clear that the armies of John of Gaunt and Jean of Brittany, now combined under the Englishman's command, crossed the Avallonnais and County of Nevers from north to south, then entered the Bourbonnais. Some of the raiders still seem to have been operating as detached units, one group causing such damage near Bourbon-Lancy on the eastern side of the river Loire that the desperate local inhabitants were given the privilege of selling their remaining produce inside the castle.

According to the *Grandes Chroniques de France*, 'The English now had little provisions . . . They had lost many of their men and most of their horses'.[29] Meanwhile the Duke of Burgundy and his troops still hovered not far away. He halted for three nights at Premery, then for three at Decize. There he was relaxed enough to play a dice game called Le Normandel, losing 400 francs to a knight named Jehan Sauvegrain. His men were also able to play *dès* and, more importantly, to rest their horses. The Constable, Bertrand du Guesclin, also appears to have been at Decize but his deputy, De Clisson, was not. In fact the Duke of Burgundy sent progress reports to De Clisson and to the Duke of Anjou while his sergeant-at-arms, Jean Pillart, carried another to King Charles.

Perhaps fearing that the Great Chevauchée now intended to invade the Rhône valley and possibly even attack the great city of Lyon, the Duke of Burgundy assembled his now rested troops and hurried ahead of the enemy's expected route, crossing the Loire at Roanne, which he reached on 11 October. The Great Chevauchée also increased its pace but crossed the river Loire further north, near Marcigny-les-Nonnains, seized and plundered the area between Putay and Diou on 12 October then headed west towards the river Allier.

This move unexpectedly threatened the regions of the Bourbonnais and Berry. Perhaps John of Gaunt now felt trapped and hoped to escape across the upper reaches of the river Cher towards Bordeaux. What is clear is that the crossing of the rivers Loire and Allier at that time of year caused the loss of most of the Great Chevauchée's baggage train and transport. At the same

---

29 Anon. (R. Delachenal ed.), *Les Grandes Chroniques de France, Chronique des Règnes de Jean II et de Charles V*, Paris (1916), pp.171–172

The Château de Billy was one of the most important fortresses in the Bourbonnais region of central France. Largely dating from the 12th and 13th centuries, a massive entrance tower was added in the later 14th century. The Great Chevauchée would have passed within sight of its walls. (Author's photograph)

time, the fact that the enemy had left Burgundian territory did not mean that the Duke of Burgundy lost interest in them. During the latter part of October his men continued to harass the Great Chevauchée, part or perhaps all of which was now heading towards Montluçon. He also sent letters warning his brother, the Duke of Berry, who is known to have been at Châtellerault on 24 October. In fact the 'bon duc' Louis II of Bourbon now seems to have taken the lead in confronting the invaders and for almost a month barred the passage of the river Allier from his headquarters at Vichy. Baulked here, John of Gaunt headed north, down the Allier towards Moulins where he was faced by Constable Du Guesclin around 22–23 October. The fighting appears to have been fierce, for only two weeks later the Duke of Bourbon gave orders for emergency repairs to the city's walls and gates. Less well-protected open villages in the fertile countryside between the Loire and Allier rivers suffered worse, including Ceron near Bourg le Comte, Bessay and Villeneuve. The last of these was burned to the ground and remained uninhabitable and religious services ceased for a long time. Duke Louis II of Bourbon rebuilt the church in 1380 and the hospital was rebuilt 15 years later, but the castle of Villeneuve was never restored.

Although we know exactly where the Duke of Burgundy was every night of the year, the location of the Great Chevauchée now becomes less clear. A brief passage in the *Grandes Chroniques de France* is particularly difficult to reconcile with other sources, suggesting that the English crossed the river Cher around 1 November, camped near Montluçon, then headed for

The Great Chevauchée is thought to have crossed the river Allier here, at Billy. This crossing, and that of the river Loire only a few days earlier, cost the invaders the bulk of their booty, most of their transport and many of their horses. (Author's photograph)

Bordeaux. This was certainly not the route taken by the main force, which reportedly crossed the Allier between Pont-du-Château and Maringues on or before 2 November. Maybe the enemy again divided into two columns or perhaps elements were now breaking away to strike out on their own. It has, in fact, been suggested that some raiders were still in the Bourbonnais area as late as 12 November, if not beyond, by which time the Duke of Burgundy had abandoned shadowing his enemies and had handed over responsibility to others.

In the meantime the Duke of Burgundy continued to watch the Great Chevauchée and to keep his brother dukes informed of developments. For example he spent four days at Souvigny discussing the military situation with the Duke of Bourbon, brother of the Queen of France, and from there, on 21 October, he sent heralds-at-arms in three different directions, 'to raise and encourage all manner of men-at-arms to fight and pursue the enemies of the king'. Other messages around this time were sent from Saint-Pourçain, where the Duke of Burgundy spent the nights of 25 to 30 October; one was addressed to the Duke of Anjou at Bourges, one to the Pope in Avignon and a third to the Constable Du Guesclin who was believed to be at Moulins. The Duke of Burgundy then headed for Aigueperse, where he spent the next three nights, followed by two and five nights at Riom and Clermont-Ferrand respectively.

With the Great Chevauchée still apparently threatening the Bourbonnais and Berry regions, the Duke of Berry also sent a report to his brother, the Duke of Anjou. This time the French communications system faltered because the recipient was wrongly thought to be at Orléans. The messenger eventually found him at Corbeil on 22 October. Four days earlier the king had nominated the Duke of Anjou as his lieutenant-general in Brittany, largely as a political move to please the Bretons because the Duke had married a daughter of a previous claimant to the Duchy, Jeanne de Penthièvre. In fact the Duke of Anjou continued to spend most of his time campaigning against the English in Aquitaine.

Meanwhile the Duke of Berry was getting impatient and wrote directly to King Charles on 20 October and, to be on safe side, ordered the *chatelains* of Niort and Poitiers to bring additional supplies of food into the fortified

21 SEPTEMBER 1373

English reach Troyes

In summer the dramatic scenery of the Puy-de-Dôme is now a major tourist attraction, but in winter this terrain can be snowbound and its weather ferocious. The winter of 1373–74, when the Great Chevauchée struggled through these highlands, is known to have been particularly wet and was followed by significant flooding of many areas. (Author's photograph)

towns along with the people of the surrounding villages. Further urgent messages went to and fro almost daily between the Duke of Berry at Châtellerault and officials in his ducal capital of Bourges, which enabled him to follow events closely. The fact that the Great Chevauchée's movements were being watched so closely might have been why John of Gaunt decided to head for Bordeaux, across the much harsher terrain of the Combrailles and what is today the *département* of Corrèze. Things certainly started badly, with the invaders losing almost all their wagons and baggage when they forced the passage of the Allier at the start of November. This equipment was then looted by the French. Meanwhile the local inhabitants also suffered severely, and even six years later the villagers of Luzillat near Maringues demanded rebates in their contributions to the war effort as a result of 'the great damage and loss their suffered because of the Duke of Lancaster and his company, which passed from their parish'.

Once again the *Grandes Chroniques* provides interesting fragments of seemingly unrelated information, which could highlight the difficulties that the Great Chevauchée would face. It noted, for example, that the following January and February there was severe flooding along several rivers that had their sources in central France. This was so bad that it caused great damage and loss of life, and almost certainly stemmed from a particularly harsh or at least wet winter in the highlands.[30] We do not know whether the Duke of Burgundy was listening to local advisers when he concluded that the Great Chevauchée was now doomed. What is known is that he decided not to pursue the invaders across the mountains but instead headed north in search of his 'war treasurer', Jean le Mercier, to obtain urgently needed cash. It had been a long campaign and his men needed payment before being discharged for the winter. The Duke of Burgundy therefore travelled to Bourges before making his way home.

John of Gaunt's march through the Auvergne clearly took that area by surprise and his decision to cross the highest mountains in central France similarly came as a surprise to those on the other side, both French and perhaps English. In fact, the Great Chevauchée's route took it westward from Clermont, between the volcanic peaks of the Puy de Dôme and Le Mont Dore, then across very rugged country towards Ussel and Tulle. This was a cold and barren land in winter, offering virtually nothing worth pillaging or indeed eating. Froissart is unfortunately reticent about this part of the campaign because there were no knightly deeds of arms to tell. He did, however, note that there was a time when the English went five days without bread. In fact they suffered a great deal more than mere hunger. The army was struck by dysentery and other diseases. It had already lost most of its baggage train and many animals while crossing the Loire and Allier rivers. Now the remaining animals began to fail and many knights had to march on foot.

The paucity of the sources leaves open the possibility that a substantial part of the Great Chevauchée had again separated from the main force before John of Gaunt turned westward, instead heading south from Clermont-

---

30 Anon. (R. Delachenal ed.), *Les Grandes Chroniques de France*, pp.173–74

Ferrand, up the headwaters of the Allier and Alagnon rivers before crossing the watershed via the Cère Pass towards Aurillac. On the other hand the only real evidence for this is the presence of 'English' at Montsalvy and Mur-de-Barrez who are more likely to have been *routiers* or a freelance 'company', which had been operating in the area for some time, rather than a breakaway element of the Great Chevauchée.

This information comes from a report, dated 14 December, from the French *consuls* or town authorities of Entraygues, and Jean de Ténières, who appears to have been the Captain of Espalion. In it they warned their colleagues in Millau that these 'English' intended to ravage the Rouergue region and advised them to guard their walls well. The report is said to have caused widespread fear and the abandonment of villages. English or pro-English elements were certainly still operating in this part of France, and are known still to have been in control of the town of Figeac. So the possibility of the Great Chevauchée combining with these remnants of English authority was real and dangerous. The fact that the Preaching Friars had to rebuild their church at Rodez in 1375 confirms the widespread devastation in this region caused by bands of roving companies, freelance and otherwise, over many years.

Part of the valley of the river Truyère is today flooded by a man-made reservoir. Yet the difficulty of this narrow, steep terrain is still clear and in the final weeks of 1373 part of the Great Chevauchée probably made its painful way down this valley towards what remained of English-ruled Aquitaine. (Author's photograph)

In fact John of Gaunt led his men across the southern Marche region in mid-November, towards the almost as rugged Limousin. The first town they reached was Ussel, which may itself still have been held by an English garrison or more likely pro-English *routiers*, despite a supposed French reconquest of this region earlier in the year. A few days later the army reached Tulle, which was certainly in French hands. Nevertheless, after some negotiations the town opened its gates, which indicates that, however battered it now was, the Great Chevauchée was still a force to be reckoned with. The exhausted soldiers were also able to obtain some food for themselves and their remaining animals. They then took the castle of Maumont, the first reasonably permanent reconquest 'by arms' of the entire campaign.

The evidence also seems to suggest that Duke Jean of Brittany either negotiated the surrender of Tulle or took control once the keys had been handed over. He was clearly blamed for making such exorbitant demands on the inhabitants that, after Tulle was retaken by the French, it was unable to pay taxes to King Charles V for many years. The next town to be reached was Brive-la-Gaillarde, which opened its gates willingly, not apparently having lost its old pro-Plantagenet, pro-English sentiment. As a result its people would later be accused of being traitors to the King of France. There is no mention of the Duke of Brittany during the reconquest of Brive. On the contrary, it seems to have been at Tulle or Brive that tensions between the two commanders of the Great Chevauchée finally reached breaking point. According to one chronicler, Guillaume de

John of Gaunt and his army crossed the watershed west of Clermont-Ferrand during the first week of November 1373. They probably took the same route as the modern main road just north of the Mont Dore, seen here, though another group might have swung south across the Col du Cère towards Aurillac. (Author's photograph)

St André, they disagreed about the payment of their troops, though in reality it is more likely to have resulted from Jean of Brittany's pretentions in this region of Limousin.

According to the *Chronique du Bon Duc Loys*, John of Gaunt now held a review of his army. Of the supposedly 15,000 men who had marched out of Calais, 8,000 remained, only half of whom still had horses, while virtually all their baggage and loot had been left by the roadside. On the other hand it is clear that the English still had prisoners, presumably men of high ransom value.

South of Brive, the strongly fortified large village or small town of Martel was also retaken by the English, along with some other minor places. Although these successes were little recompense for the huge expenditure and effort of the Great Chevauchée, they might have given John of Gaunt confidence to send an embassy to Pope Gregory XI early in December, urging a revival of peace negotiations. This mission probably travelled southwards towards Toulouse and then along the coast to the papal enclave of Avignon.

Another illustration from the *Décades de Tite-Live*, dating from the reign of King Charles V, shows military leaders in apparent disagreement. Strains between John of Gaunt and his ally Jean IV de Montfort, the nominal Duke of Brittany, had clearly emerged by the time the Great Chevauchée crossed the Haute-Auvergne in winter. (Bibliothèque Municipale, Ms. 730, Bordeaux)

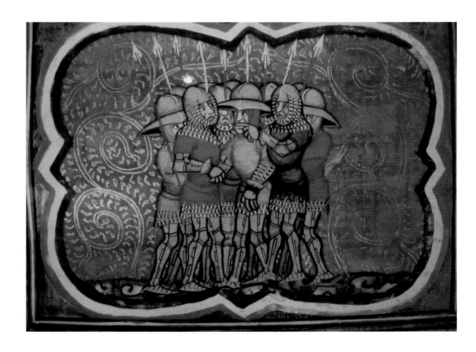

In fact the French were relieved rather than triumphant, and their chroniclers were unstinting in their admiration for the epic courage shown by the English on the Great Chevauchée. Nor were they yet convinced that the danger had completely passed. While the invaders were making their painful way across the highlands and down towards the Dordogne valley, the Duke of Berry had returned to Poitiers during the first week of November. There he and his troops remained on guard and read reports of the enemy's progress with care. His wife, Jeanne d'Armagnac, was now getting increasingly worried and sent a letter by her personal messenger, 'the faithful Pellerin', on 5 November, demanding a prompt response. Henpecked or genuinely concerned, the Duke of Berry hurriedly returned home where he remained for the rest of the month. In fact the threat had passed and this enabled the three ducal brothers of Berry, Anjou and Burgundy to meet and discuss the following year's operations against the English.

The dukes also had family and political affairs to discuss following the death of their sister Jehanne de France, wife of the King of Navarre, on 3 November at Evreux. Four days later Cardinal Etienne of Paris died in Avignon and Jehan de Dormans, the Cardinal of Beauvais who had long been the Chancellor of France, also died in Paris. The ducal brothers then returned to their various administrative and military duties, though the Duke of Berry and the Duke of Burgundy first went to Paris for discussions with their brother the King. Burgundy then went home, but in January his infant son, Charles Monsieur, fell gravely ill and his parents sent messages to major churches across the land asking for prayers to be said for the child. Charles Monsieur nevertheless died at Rouvre during the night of 11–12 July 1374.

Berry was more fortunate, rejoining his wife at Saint-Pourçain in the Auvergne early in January 1374. However, there still seems to have been fighting in central France. The enemy remains obscure, but 'about fifteen days before Christmas' there was an 'affray' in which 'all the men at arms of the country' took part in order to expel 'our enemies'. The town of Châtillon-sur-Cher was somehow involved and was subsequently sent a royal 'letter of remission', excusing some taxes because of the great harm and damage that had been done.[31]

After leaving Brive-la-Gaillarde, and probably now without Duke Jean of Brittany's contingent, John of Gaunt's army marched to the river Dordogne.

Even in summer the uplands of the Auvergne can seem a little forbidding. If part of the Great Chevauchée did head further south towards the Rouergue area, as some sources suggest, then it would have trudged past Clemensat towards the Monts du Cantal. (Author's photograph)

31 Lehoux, F., *Jean de France, Duc de Berri, sa Vie, son Action Politique (1340–1416), vol. 1, De la Naissance de Jean de France à la Mort de Charles V*, Paris (1966), p.317–18

The Great Chevauchée had some siege equipment at the start of its great raid, but no apparent attempt was made to attack fortified towns or even substantial castles as the invaders made their way across central France. Fortunately this fortress of Castelnaud was in friendly hands when the hungry, disease-ridden invaders arrived beneath its walls. (Fred Nicolle's photograph)

Again their exact route is unclear, but they seem more likely to have cut across the limestone plateau of the Périgord Noir to Souillac or Sarlat rather than going down the narrow and winding valley of the river Vézère. The English were now in largely friendly territory, though some castles were held by lords loyal to King Charles V. The great fortress of Beynac, on the north bank of the Dordogne near Sarlat, had been allocated to the English crown in the Treaty of Brétigny with its *chatelain* as a vassal of the Bishop of Sarlat. But in 1368, even before the formal resumption of the Hundred Years War, Pons IV de Beynac threw off English suzereinty and declared himself for King Charles V. Throughout the subsequent conflict he remained loyal to the French crown, even when the Great Chevauchée marched right past his door.

Facing Beynac from the other side of the Dordogne was another equally powerful castle, that of Castelnaud, which is understood to have been in pro-English hands. This may have been why the Great Chevauchée apparently crossed to the southern bank. John of Gaunt next occupied Limeuil by agreement, its lord, Nicholas de Beaufort, being the Pope's brother, but was obliged to retake Lalinde by force. From then on the remnants of the Great Chevauchée were clearly in friendly soil, the town of Bergerac actually being one of John of Gaunt's own feudal possessions. Here the army crossed the Dordogne by a great medieval bridge whose southern end is currently being studied by French archaeologists.

The road from Bergerac to Bordeaux, lying south of the Dordogne, was through relatively secure territory. Nevertheless, when John of Gaunt and his followers finally marched into Bordeaux on Christmas Eve 1373, they were a half-starved and bedraggled crew, though they are still said to have behaved with discipline. The Great Chevauchée was finally over. According to the *Grandes Chroniques de France*, 'They had lost most of their men and it is believed there were more than 1,000 knights now on foot, who had lost their armours, some thrown into rivers, others cast aside because they could not carry them. And because the French would not help them I think that this chevauchée was the most honourable [such campaign], but to them the most damaging.'[32]

---

32 Anon. (R. Delachenal ed.), *Les Grandes Chroniques de France*, pp.171–72.

ANALYSIS

The Great Chevauchée had marched almost 900km from Calais to Bordeaux, and had lost about a third of its men, including desertions, and almost all of its animals. Widespread devastation had been caused but there had been no significant battle against the French, and certainly no major victory. On the other hand friends and foes generally agreed that the whole thing had been hugely heroic and a most 'noble feat of arms'. Whether the Great Chevauchée had enhanced John of Gaunt's prestige outside a small circle of men like the chronicler Froissart, who were clearly impressed by such things, remains doubtful.

Events in Bordeaux in the weeks following the Great Chevauchée's arrival suggest that many in his own army were disillusioned. He clearly had difficulty paying them and in maintaining discipline while the greatly reduced territory still under English control in Aquitaine was hardly in position to help. According to the *Anonimalle Chronicler* the soldiers could not obtain enough food for themselves nor fodder for their horses. The fact that John of Gaunt found it necessary to forbid them from taking what they needed without payment suggests that many were trying to do so. It seems that many men as well as animals now died, probably too hungry and weak to resist the sickness that had already ravaged their ranks.

Some ordinary soldiers petitioned their leaders either to lead them against enemy territory or to allow them to go home. Both requests were refused. Yet sufficient men purchased their own passage to England for King Edward III to order the Mayor and Sheriffs of London to arrest all those who returned without from Aquitaine without a licence. The order was expressed in terms of the dishonour, breaking of faith and contempt for royal authority that such desertion entailed. Meanwhile, in Bordeaux even knights were reduced to begging 'poorly arrayed and attired', which was seen as a disgrace both to them and to their comrades. Of course the leaders were also in financial difficulty, John of Gaunt extracting substantial loans from the Church authorities of the Cathedral of Saint-André in Bordeaux and from others.

When John of Gaunt arrived at Bergerac he was entering a town that belonged to him personally and was also strategically important because of its bridge across the Dordogne. Only the southern end of this medieval structure remains, and is currently being studied by archaeologists. (Author's photograph)

In February 1374 Duke Jean of Brittany sailed from Bordeaux to Brittany, where three fortresses remained loyal to him; Derval, Brest and Auray. John of Gaunt was meanwhile appalled by the situation in what remained of English Aquitaine, having 'found the country in a great mischief everywhere'. Despite desertions and sickness, he nevertheless still had a useful army in Bordeaux with which he hoped to reverse the situation once campaigning could start again in spring. This he managed to do, if only on a limited scale, by regaining a few frontier towns and castles. Even before the fighting restarted, John of Gaunt sent an embassy to seek an alliance with Peter III of Aragon. However, his biggest diplomatic coup was getting Gaston Fébus, the Count of Foix, to abandon his neutrality and ally himself with the English crown.

These successes so alarmed the Duke of Anjou that he persuaded King Enrique of Castile to bring a large army over the Pyrenees to help him. The two sides even agreed on the day for a great battle near Moissac, though this eventually had to be postponed because another truce came into effect. By then the French under the Duke of Anjou had launched their own offensive, having mustered a substantial army in the Périgord area that included many Genoese crossbowmen. This he led into Upper Gascony where they achieved considerable success.

Meanwhile the Pope in Avignon was still trying to encourage peace negotiations, selecting the (nominal) Patriarch of Jerusalem and the Archbishop of Bordeaux, whose positions were confirmed in a letter dated 6 March 1374. This time they found greater willingness to accept their mediation efforts, partly through threats of excommunication but mostly because both sides were exhausted by war. Plague and famine had also returned to southern France, especially Gascony.

Eventually a truce was agreed with the French Constable, Bertrand du Guesclin, while John of Gaunt prepared to hand over command in Aquitaine to Sir Thomas Felton. Charles V, however, was reluctant to confirm Du Guesclin's truce, though Froissart claimed that 'a truce was agreed upon between the Dukes of Anjou and Lancaster (John of Gaunt) and their allies, until the last day of August; and they engaged themselves to be, in the month of September, in the country of Picardy – the Duke of Anjou at St. Omer, and the Duke of Lancaster at Calais'. This was so that they could resume the struggle in a proper knightly fashion.[33] Apparently this truce was also arranged with the agreement of the King of England.

Between the Great Chevauchée's arrival in Bordeaux, and John of Gaunt's departure in April 1374, an exchange or mutual ransoming of prisoners had to be sorted out. Comparable arrangements had probably been agreed during the course of the campaign and it is impossible to state with certainty when various captives were released. The names of only the most senior are known and on the French side they included Odinet de Chazeron, the Duke of Burgundy's 'bread store keeper', who had to pay a large ransom but was given 200 gold *deniers* towards this sum by the Duke. Jean Disque, the Duke's stable squire, had been taken prisoner near Troyes but was similarly given 100 gold *francs* towards his ransom, while Jean de Bourgogne-Comté's trumpeter and several important figures had been captured by the English in the vicinity of Moulins. The French, and especially the Burgundians, has also taken prisoners. For example, Geoffroi the Bastard of Charny had sold a notable English knight, Guillaume Bouson, to the Duke for 500 *livres*. Jean de Ray and Guillaume the Bastard of Poitiers tried to make a similar arrangement for their important English prisoner, 'a most valliant knight' named Mathieu de Gournay. The Earl of Pembroke and many others captured by the Castilian fleet during battle of La Rochelle in 1372 seem to have been ransomed and released while the Great Chevauchée was making its way across France.

Amongst John of Gaunt's final acts before leaving Bordeaux for England was to sign an indenture on 4 April 1374, agreeing to pay John Cresswell and Geoffrey St Quinteyn 6,000 florins of Avignon for 'keeping the castle' of Lusignan, or more correctly to continue to defend it, until 1 September. Lusignan was an important, if now very isolated, position on the road between Niort and Poitiers and was one of the few such castles still held by pro-English forces.

24 DECEMBER 1373

John of Gaunt and his men enter Bordeaux

As English power collapsed in Aquitaine, French authority did not replace it in an even manner. When the Great Chevauchée reached the Dordogne valley it reoccupied Limeuil by agreement with its lord, Nicholas de Beaufort, who was the Pope's brother, but it had to retake the vital river crossing of Lalinde, seen here, by force. (Author's photograph)

---

33 Froissart, Jean (anon. tr.), *The Chronicles of England, France and Spain*, London (1906), pp.141–44

By the time John of Gaunt had sailed back to England, the truth about his disastrous campaign was known. While the campaign was under way Sir John Knyvett, King Edward III's Chancellor, had assured Parliament that John of Gaunt's forces had 'stayed the malice of the King's adversaries and by their good and noble governance and deeds of arms had wrought great damage and destruction to the enemy in France'. By November 1373, however, Parliament was expressing anger about the campaign, news of which was filtering back to England. The king was old and frail, his eldest and most famous son the Black Prince was clearly unwell, the House of Commons was getting restless and, in the words of a 20th-century historian, 'An overtaxed and leaderless people, at once war-weary and bellicose, were becoming ripe for revolt'.[34]

John of Gaunt's Great Chevauchée was the last big English campaign of the 1370s and its leader had a lot of explaining to do when he got home; not least why at least one third of his men had been lost to various causes and 30,000 expensive horses had similarly failed to reach Bordeaux. On the other hand the sheer epic of the Great Chevauchée raised England's military prestige for a while. Paradoxically, this was most obvious amongst its French opponents, the *Grandes Chroniques* describing it as 'most honourable to the English'.

In an age that often admired courage above success, the expedition also enhanced John of Gaunt's own military credentials. In practical terms he had managed to bring much needed reinforcements to Aquitaine and for a short while halted the French reconquest. Some have suggested that he had also taken pressure off the English garrisons and their allies in Brittany, but the facts do not support such a view.

Both sides could also be said to have failed in several respects. For England, there had been no major military gain to compensate for the huge effort and expenditure of the Great Chevauchée. The Plantagenet English King Edward III was no closer to winning the French throne, which he had so long claimed, and a substantial English army had been virtually destroyed piecemeal. On the French side, a victory of sorts had been won without much loss of blood or treasure, but also without any glory. Duke Philip the Bold of Burgundy had undeniably distinguished himself, but more by caution, restraint and strategic skill than through success on the battlefield. This hardly increased his prestige in the cultural context of the 14th century, though a 21st-century observer might see him as an undoubtedly superior military leader compared to his opponents. Under his command Jean de Vienne and Jean de Bueil had inflicted several defeats upon the English, notably at Oulchy-le-Château, while between Sens and Joigny, Olivier de Clisson showed the skill that would justify his later succeeding Bertrand du Guesclin as Constable of France.

In military terms, the last word could be given to a more recent British military historian: 'By the end of 1374 the French had reduced English Aquitaine to a mere strip along the Biscay coast from Bordeaux to Bayonne . . . In the north, England held on to Calais and Cherbourg, while in Brittany she retained only Brest and Auray. With the exception of these ports along

---

34 McKisack, M., *The Oxford History of England, vol. 5, The Fourteenth Century 1307–1399*, Oxford (1959), p.385

Hunger, exposure and diseases such as dysentery took a much higher toll of the Great Chevauchée than did battlefield casualties. Nevertheless, many had been injured or killed and some may have found refuge in monasteries, like the wounded knight in this late 14th-century French manuscript. (Bibliothèque National, Ms. Fr.343, f.7r, Paris)

the French seaboard, all Edward III's gains in his long war with France were reduced to less than he had held when the conflict began, and none of his political ambitions had been achieved'.[35]

The Great Chevauchée had certainly been expensive, costing the government well over £82,000 for wages and shipping across the Channel, plus a further £14,000 in gifts or loans – in reality, bribes – to Duke Jean of Brittany. Its failure probably resulted from an English unwillingness to recognize that chevauchées could no longer achieve the results they had during the early part of the Hundred Years War. This was an unpalatable fact for knights, squires and other professional soldiers who still expected to make their fortune out of such raids. Defensive operations that produced little or no booty, especially those within friendly territory, were far less attractive and as a result it was much more difficult to raise armies of volunteers. Professionals could be paid to undertake less lucrative campaigns, but they were very expensive to hire.

35 Peter Reid, *A Brief History of Medieval Warfare: The Rise and Fall of English Supremacy at Arms, 1314–1485*, London (2008), pp.163–65

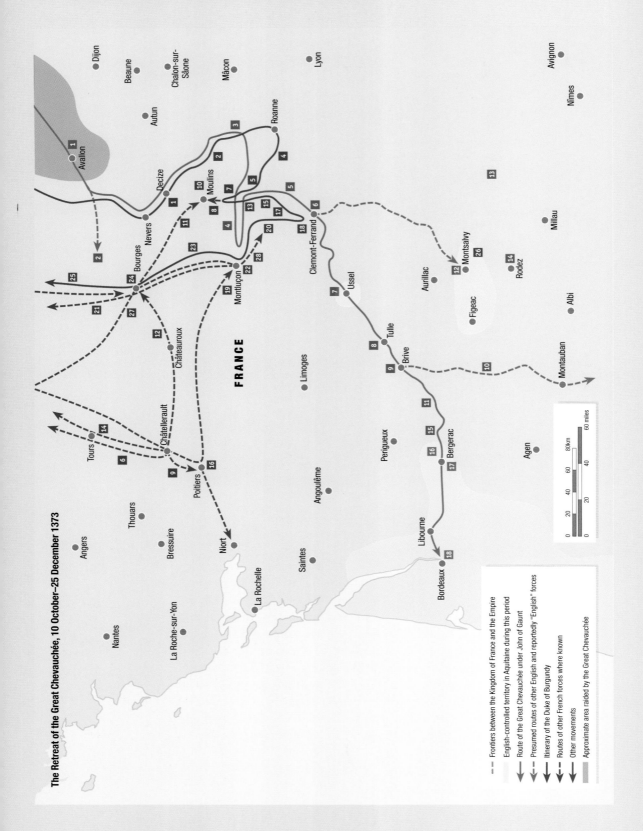

The Retreat of the Great Chevauchée, 10 October–25 December 1373

F R A N C E

Dijon

Beaune

Chalon-sur-Sâone

Mâcon

Lyon

Avignon

Nîmes

Autun

Roanne

Avallon

Decize

Moulins

Nevers

Bourges

Châteauroux

Clemont-Ferrand

Montsalvy

Millau

Rodez

Albi

Montauban

Aurillac

Figeac

Ussel

Tulle

Brive

Limoges

Periqueux

Bergerac

Agen

Châtellerault

Poitiers

Tours

Niort

Angoulême

Saintes

La Rochelle

Libourne

Bordeaux

Thouars

Angers

Bressuire

Nantes

La Roche-sur-Yon

Montluçon

- - - Frontiers between the Kingdom of France and the Empire

English-controlled territory in Aquitaine during this period

Route of the Great Chevauchée under John of Gaunt

Presumed routes of other English and reportedly "English" forces

Itinerary of the Duke of Burgundy

Routes of other French forces where known

Other movements

Approximate area raided by the Great Chevauchée

0   20   40   60   80/km
0   20   40   60 miles

THE RETREAT OF THE GREAT CHEVAUCHÉE, 10 OCTOBER–25 DECEMBER 1373

■ Key to English and allied movements

1 Great Chevauchée ravaging Avallon area (first week of October)
2 Elements of the Great Chevauchée possibly raiding the Bourbonnais (mid-October to mid-November)
3 Great Chevauchée crosses the Loire at Marcigny, losing considerable baggage, transport and booty in the process
4 Great Chevauchée crosses the Allier at Billy, losing most of its remaining baggage, booty and many horses; elements said to include John of Gaunt then reported near Montluçon, perhaps making a tentative move westwards (end October–early November)
5 Great Chevauchée under John of Gaunt abandons presumed plan to reach Bordeaux through the Bourbonnais and Berry; instead moves towards the Auvergne (late October–early November)
6 Main body of the Great Chevauchée crosses Auvergne watershed via the Combrailles, west of Clermont-Ferrand, heading for Tulle (first week of November)
7 Great Chevauchée passes through upper Limousin, through Ussel which was apparently still held by an English garrison or 'pro-English' routiers (mid-November)
8 Great Chevauchée reaches Tulle which opens its gates after prolonged negotiation; clear rupture between John of Gaunt and Jean of Brittany around this time (late November)
9 Great Chevauchée reaches Brive which opens its gates and declares for the English cause, along with some other small towns; Great Chevauchée also captures the French-held castle of Maumont; John of Gaunt holds a review of his remaining troops (mid-December)
10 John of Gaunt sends an embassy from Brive to the Pope in Avignon, probably via Toulouse, to encourage a renewal of peace negotiations
11 Great Chevauchée occupies Sarlat
12 'English' reported at Montsalvy and Mur-de-Barrez preparing to ravage the Rouergue region, either a group which broke away from the Great Chevauchée or a freelance 'company' operating in this area for some time (14 December); note English still controlled Figeac
13 'English' still operating in the Gévaudin area
14 'Companies' devastate the church of the Preaching Friars at Rodez around this period
15 Great Chevauchée occupies Limeuil by agreement with its lord, Nicholas de Beaufort, brother of the Pope
16 Great Chevauchée takes Lalinde by force
17 Great Chevauchée enters English-held Bergerac (probably third week of December)
18 Great Chevauchée reaches Bordeaux (24 December)

■ Key to French movements

1 Duke of Burgundy at Decize (7–9 October)
2 Duke of Burgundy 'camping in the countryside' (10 October)
3 Duke of Burgundy at Roanne (11–12 October)
4 Duke of Burgundy at Saint-Hoan-le-Châtel (13 October)
5 Duke of Burgundy probably at Cusset (14–17 October)
6 Duke of Berry at Châtellerault, sends messages to Charles V and the Duke of Anjou who were thought to be at Orléans (actually in or on their way to Corbeil), warning that the Great Chevauchée endangers the Bourbonnais and Berry areas (16 October)
7 Duke of Burgundy at Saint-Pourçain (18 October)
8 Duke of Burgundy at Souvigny, discusses strategy with the Duke of Bourbon who has probably been with him since leaving Troyes (19–23 October); Duke of Burgundy also sends heralds 'in three directions' to raise troops to fight the Great Chevauchée (21 October)
9 Duke of Berry sends a further message to Charles V; also orders chatelains of Niort and Poitiers to bring food and people from surrounding villages into the fortified towns, then leaves for Paris (20 October)
10 Duke of Bourbon remains to defend his own domain, probably joining or awaiting the Duke of Anjou at Moulins (24 October)
11 Duke of Anjou arrives in Moulins (late October)
12 Urgent messages to and fro between the Duke of Berry at Châtellerault and Bourges, on the threat to Berry and the Bourbonnais posed by the Great Chevauchée (last week October)
13 Duke of Burgundy returns to establish HQ at Saint-Pourçain (25–30 October)
14 Duke of Berry leaves Châtellerault and travels to Paris to discuss the situation with King Charles V (by 30 October)
15 Duke of Burgundy moves HQ to Aigueperse (31 October–2 November)
16 Duke of Berry returns to Poitiers where he remains about one week (early November)
17 Duke of Burgundy moves to Riom (3–4 November)
18 Duke of Burgundy at Clermont-Ferrand (5–9 November), decides that the Great Chevauchée is no longer a threat so heads north to find his 'war treasurer', Jean le Mercier, for funds to pay troops
19 Duke of Berry heads for Berry, still fearing a thrust by the Great Chevauchée (around 7 November)
20 Duke of Burgundy at Aigueperse, heading north (10 November)
21 Duke of Berry reportedly in Paris (mid- to end November); having passed through Montluçon (around 11 November)
22 Duke of Burgundy at 'Molisson', probably Montluçon, meeting the Duke of Anjou and Duke of Berry (11–14 November)
23 Dukes of Burgundy and Anjou at Ainay (15 November)
24 Dukes of Burgundy and Anjou in Bourges (16–17 November)
25 Dukes of Burgundy and Anjou at Aubigny (18 November); continue to Sens to attend funeral mass for Queen Jeanne, sister of Charles V (29 November)
26 Consuls of Entraygues and Jean de Ténières of Espalion warn the consuls of Millau that there are "English" at Montsalvy and Mur-le-Barrez (14 November)
27 Duke of Berry returns to Bourges (early December); attends another mass for the soul of his sister Jeanne (19 December)
28 Duke of Berry goes to the Auvergne (late December); then rejoins his wife as Saint-Pourçain (early January 1374)

CONCLUSION

The Great Chevauchée is not seen as one of the main events of the Hundred Years War, though it could be regarded as marking a significant turning point. Within a few years it would be overshadowed by developments that had a far more profound impact upon French, English and indeed European history, most notably the Papal Schism of 1378. Even within the context of the Hundred Years War subsequent developments soon reduced John of Gaunt's epic campaign from the Channel coast to the Bay of Biscay to something of a sideshow. There would, in fact, be little campaigning on land after 1380, and following a series of short truces an agreement was signed in 1396 under which both England and France accepted the status quo.

This more permanent truce still left the main questions unresolved and, a generation later, the Hundred Years War would break out again and be marked by another overwhelming English victory at the battle of Agincourt in 1415. Like Crécy and Poitiers earlier, success at Agincourt would nevertheless prove illusory and within less than half a century the Hundred Years War would finally end with a French victory.

In more immediate terms the Great Chevauchée's lack of success caused great anger in England, where people had become accustomed to victory. John of Gaunt's elder brother, the Black Prince, died in 1376, followed by his father King Edward III the following year. By then John of Gaunt wielded considerable political power and continued to do so under the new king, Richard II. Yet he never managed to win real popularity, and even his efforts to promote peace with France did not find universal approval. According to Froissart, the Duke of Gloucester objected to Anglo-French peace in 1390 on the grounds of its effects on 'poor knights and squires and archers of England whose comforts and station in society depend upon war'. Similar attitudes were found in Gascony, where many relied on war against other Frenchmen for their living. It seemed that the unfortunate John of Gaunt could never win.

In France the containment if not defeat of the Great Chevauchée was just one more step in a military and political process that saw the English confined to a few small coastal enclaves by the time of the 1396 truce.

There are still many relics of English rule in Bordeaux. For example, the decoratively carved north door of the Cathedral of Saint-André dates from the late 14th-century when the remnants of the once huge domain won by King Edward III early in the Hundred Years War were shrinking to little more than the city and its immediate surroundings. (Author's photograph)

The impact of decades of war should not, however, be exaggerated even within France. Here it is clear that war killed far fewer people than did the plague. On the other hand the structural damage, particularly that caused by English chevauchées, was clearly extensive. This can be seen in a little-known work by P.H. Denifle, largely based upon Vatican archives and published in 1899, analysing damage to Church property. Its second volume deals with the period up to the death of Charles V and shows that 1373 was not a particularly bad year.[36] In political terms, the military demands of the Hundred Years War led to increased government centralization in later 14th-century France. At the same time, however, the later years of King Charles V's reign, and more particularly that of his successor Charles VI, witnessed that increased factionalism amongst the ruling elite which would bring disaster upon France early in the following century.

---

36 Denifle, P.H., *La Guerre de Cent and et la Désolation des Eglises, Monastères et Hôpitaux en France: Jusqu'à la Mort de Charles V (1380)* (Paris 1899, reprint Brussels 1965).

BIBLIOGRAPHY

General histories of the Hundred Years War, which naturally include the Great Chevauchée, are not included here.

Anon. (R. Delachenal ed.), *Les Grandes Chroniques de France, Chronique des Règnes de Jean II et de Charles V*, Paris (1916)

Armitage-Smith, S., *John of Gaunt*, London (1904)

Armitage-Smith, S., *John of Gaunt's Register*, 2 vols, London (1911)

Bors, P., 'La jacquerie des Tuchins', *Histoire Médiévale*, 46 (October 2003), pp.12–17

Bruand, Y., 'La position stratégique des Châteaux du Bourbonnois au Moyen Âge', *Bulletin Monumental*, 110 (1952), pp.101–18

Calmette, J., *Charles V, King of France*, London (1945)

Chazaud, A-M., *La Chronique du Bon Duc Loys de Bourbon*, Paris (1876)

Collins, A., *The History of John of Gaunt . . .* , London (1740)

Contamine, P., 'Les fortifications urbaines en France á la fin du Moyen Age . . .', *Revue Historique*, 260 (1978), pp.23–47

Curry, A. (et al.), '1373', in *The Soldier in Later Medieval England* (2009): www.icmacentre.ac.uk/soldier/database

Denifle, P.H., *La Guerre de Cent and et la Désolation des Eglises, Monastères et Hôpitaux en France: Jusqu'à la Mort de Charles V (1380)* (Paris 1899, reprint Brussels 1965)

Fournier, G., 'La defence des populations rurales pendant la Guerre de Cent Ans en Basse Auvergne', in *Actes du XCe Congrés National de Sociétés Savants*, Paris (1966), pp.157–99

Froissart, J. (anon. ed.), *The Chronicles of England, France and Spain*, London (1906): (A. Pauphilet & E. Pognon eds), 'Les Chroniques', in *Historiens et Chroniqueurs du Moyen Age*, Paris (1952); (G.T. Diller ed.), *Chroniques, Livre 1, Le Manuscrit d'Amiens*, Geneva (1993)

Given-Wilson, C., *The English Nobility in the Later Middle Ages: The Fourteenth Century Political Community*, London (1996)

Gondoin, S.W., *Hundred Years War Castles*, Paris (2007)

Goodman, A., *John of Gaunt: The Exercise of Princely Power in Fourteenth-Century Europe*, London (1992)

Henneman, J.B., *Olivier de Clisson and Political Society in France under Charles V and Charles VI*, Philadelphia (1996)

Jones, M., *Ducal Brittany, 1364–1399: Relations with England and France during the Reign of Duke John IV*, Oxford (1970)

Jones, M., *Letters, Orders and Musters of Bertrand du Guesclin, 1357–1380*, Woodbridge (2004)

Lehoux, F., *Jean de France, Duc de Berri, sa Vie, son Action Politique (1340–1416), vol. 1, De la Naissance de Jean de France à la Mort de Charles V*, Paris (1966)

McKisack, M., *The Oxford History of England, vol. 5: The Fourteenth Century 1307–1399*, Oxford (1959)

Mirot, L., & Deprez E., *Les Ambassades Anglaises pendant le Guerre de Cent Ans . . .*, Paris (1900)

Morillo, S., 'Battle Seeking: The Contexts and Limits of Vegetian Strategy', *The Journal of Medieval Military History*, 1 (2002), pp.212–42

Noel, R.P.R., *Town Defences in the French Midi during the Hundred Years War, c.1337–c.1453* (Ph.D. thesis, Edinburgh 1977)

Petit, E., *Ducs de Bourgogne de la Maison de Valois. Philippe de Hardi*, Paris (1909)

Petit, E., *Itinéraires de Philippe le Hardi et de Jean Sans Peur, Ducs de Bourgognes (1363–1419)*, Paris (1888)

Prestwich, M., *Why did Englishmen Fight in the Hundred Years War?*, London (1992)

Riley, T.H., 'Delivery of a barge, provided by the City to serve under the King, together with the riggling and tackle thereof, to William Martlesham, its master (1373)', *De Re Militari Website* (February 2009): www.deremilitari.org/resources/resources

Terrier de Loray, M., *Jean de Vienne, Amiral de France, 1341–1396*, Paris (1878)

Troubat, O., *La Guerre de Cent Ans et la Prince Chevalier le 'Bon Duc' Louis de Bourbon*, Montluçon (2001)

Vaughan, R., *Philip the Bold: The Formation of the Burgundian State*, London (1962)

Wright, N., *Knights and Peasants: The Hundred Years War in the French Countryside*, Woodbridge (1998)

INDEX

80